OCCULT
EXP_____
- *SAFELY*

Doug Harris

REACHOUT
TRUST

BUILDING A BRIDGE OF REASON

Original edition first published 2000

This revised and updated edition published 2006
by Reachout Trust, 24 Ormond Road, Richmond,
Surrey TW10 6TH

ISBN 0 9513632 4 7
978-0-95136-324-9

British Library Cataloguing Data
A catalogue record for this book is available
from the British Library

CONTENTS

SECTION 1

SECTION 2

SECTION 3

Section One

Introduction

Purpose

The main purpose of this book is to produce helpful material for Sunday School teachers, youth leaders, religious education teachers, etc. We believe it will help explain the dangers of the many different facets of the occult, to those they teach, without raising unnecessary interest in the subject. There is no reason, however, why any individual should not benefit from the clear explanations contained here.

Each section contains all the basic information needed to prepare a lesson on the particular subject.

Group Activity

At the end of each section, we have also included group activities. The purpose for these is that, through practical means, the lessons taught in the section will be reinforced.

Personal Follow-Up

This section is for the individual who needs to take the matter further either because of personal involvement in the subject or because he or she wants to help others.

Preparation

If you are taking a lesson, do prepare well beforehand, to ensure that the message comes across clearly and sensibly.

Occult Dangers Explained - *Safely*

Some of the answers in the activities at the end of each subject will draw on information found in the *Overview* (p.7) and *Conclusion* (p.127) as well. Please ensure you have these facts to hand as well as any relevant Scriptures that could be used.

Help

It could be that, with all the written information, you still have questions. Maybe when you are talking to your group questions arise that you cannot answer and if this is the case, there is help available from Reachout Trust.

You will also discover that we have further information available on the subjects covered here. Ask for our full resource list or download it from the website.

Reachout Trust
24 Ormond Road
Richmond
Surrey
TW10 6TH

Phone: 0870 770 3258
Fax: 0870 770 3259
E-mail: rt@reachouttrust.org
Web: http://www.reachouttrust.org

Acknowledgement

I would like to acknowledge two particular sources that were used in the preparation of this book. Tom Poulson and others who created the original *Christian Response to the Occult* factsheets that are now published by Reachout Trust and Kevin Logan, especially for his book *Paganism and the Occult* (Kingsway/ Reachout Trust).

Overview

We are used to warning signs in our daily lives and in many cases we accept them as being constructive. For instance, the warning of live electricity rails at the level crossing. However, it also seems to be part of human nature that, often, we choose to ignore clearly defined dangers.

Near where I live, by the River Thames, there is a clear warning sign for car drivers, "This area is liable to sudden flooding". Why do motorists ignore the sign and park their car just in that spot? Perhaps some think it is an old sign with no relevance for today. Others might feel the flooding will not happen today! Whatever the reason, regularly in spring and autumn, when the high tides come, cars are enveloped with water.

Then we have the packet of cigarettes, sold in Britain, with the bold warning, 'Smoking kills'. Those words give you a choice: totally ignore it and carry on smoking or stop and find out what evidence there is to the warning. One leading American tobacco firm has finally admitted that smoking can cause cancer, yet still millions choose to ignore the warning.

This is where we start with the occult, **"The Occult Is Potentially Dangerous"**. Individuals can, of course, choose to ignore it, but I hope all will stop long enough to ask the question, 'What is your evidence?'

Increasingly, people seem to be accepting the fact that there is evidence to back up that statement. For instance, Julie Burchill, in a newspaper article in the late 1990s showed that occult and superstition have moved into the space vacated by the retreat of traditional Judaeo-Christian belief. It went on to issue a warning:

> "Never underestimate the power of superstition; it doesn't just dope the masses, it can bring down dynasties. It was the lure of the Tarot, the personal astrologer and plastic

> pyramid which helped break up the marriages
> of both the Prince of Wales and Duke of York."

She further admitted, on a personal level that:

> "... as a Ouija worshipping pseudo-satanic
> teenager I would primly maintain that
> superstition was okay, while religion was
> wicked."

However, the article closes with the author beginning to change her mind, as she looked forward to a new millennium.

Unfortunately, this change does not appear to be the trend of all. Many, especially teenagers, seem to be finding the lure of the occult and supernatural very tempting. In a 2000 MORI poll of 2,610 young people, between the ages of 11 and 16, 54% were very or fairly interested in the occult and the supernatural. This caused the *Association of Teachers and Lecturers,* who had commissioned the poll, to issue a press statement expressing their concerns that:

> "Unsupervised access to the internet meant
> more young people would find it easy to visit
> websites dealing with the occult and
> unsavoury subjects such as bloodletting
> techniques." - *Report,* June/July 2000, p.15.

This interest by young people is illustrated by a 2004 article in a North Wales newspaper, where two reporters went undercover to expose a coven set up by young people.

> "A row has erupted over a witches' coven, set
> up in Aberystwyth by four girls under the age
> of 16. A *Cambrian News* reporter posed as a
> 14-year-old schoolgirl to expose the Silver
> Moon Coven which was trying to recruit
> members as young as 11... the father of one

of the coven members was horrified to learn…
a website… contained details of the girls,
including their young ages. The *Cambrian
News* launched its investigation after a poster
was spotted in Aberystwyth's Public Library
looking for new members, aged between 11
and 18, mainly girls, to become witches and
Wiccans. The poster has since been
removed…" - *The Cambrian News,* 22
January 2004.

What is the Occult?

The word occult means 'hidden' or 'concealed'; the opposite
of God's revelation. The meaning of 'revelation' is literally,
"taking the lid off". The occult puts it back on again.

The purpose of the various occult practices, described in
later sections, is to give an outward appearance of being one
thing but inside being something totally different. Just like
the now famous *Dr Who's* Tardis; there is an ordinary
looking doorway that opens into a three-dimensional
supernatural world.

The occult can also be likened to the joke birthday
present, beautifully wrapped outside but, once unwrapped, we
discover something nasty and horrible.

Devil or Demons?

You often hear the claim, "The Devil tempted me"; in most
cases this is not true. The Devil, although a supernatural
being, is limited to being in one place at one time. So, who
does his work for him? He has an army of demons and evil
powers under his command that do his work. This is clearly
summed up in one Bible verse:

For our struggle is not against flesh and
blood, but against rulers, against the

9

powers, against the world forces of this darkness, against the spiritual forces of wickedness in the heavenly places. - Ephesians 6:12

These supernatural beings are very real, as many will testify, and can have a harmful effect on our lives. The Bible is realistic when it says we struggle, but please note it is not against the people who are involved in these things but against the demonic forces behind the practices.

Many want to say that the devil and demons are the invention of the 'evangelical Christians', but interestingly there are a growing band of psychiatrists who believe that humans can be possessed by demons.

"For many doctors, such talk [of possession] would have been proof only of extreme mental illness, rather than a genuine paranormal encounter. Perhaps Peter was suffering from psychosis and hallucinations. But demonic possession? Surely the very idea is hokum? Not according to Dr Sanderson, a respected member of the Royal College of Psychiatrists. He believes that demonic spirits are a very real and frightening phenomenon." - *Daily Mail,* February 19 2005, p.46.

Supernatural Dangers

Among those who practice the occult, you will find some very good 'con artists.'

"Around one in five believed they were witnessing paranormal phenomena when they saw candlesticks moved by trickery and balls lifted in the air using hidden poles... believers in the paranormal had a greater tendency to report strange happenings than sceptics, who assumed they were being hoaxed... The table was covered with objects... which volunteers were asked to move using the power of thought. But two accomplices were in the room shifting the objects using string and a pole... one in three swore the table tipped. And at least 20 per cent said they felt change in temperature and unusual smells. These did not happen." - *Daily Mail*, August 15 2003, p.43

However, the true occult is supernatural, which, by very definition of the word, means that this realm is greater than the purely natural realm. We are natural beings located in time and having physical limitations. The occult powers, on the other hand, are supernatural and not limited to time or physical bodies. This is what makes them so dangerous. We feel that we are in control but in reality the supernatural powers are greater than us and are truly in control.

Getting involved with the occult can be likened to a train journey. When you decide to take the journey, you are in control. You then decide which day and which train and you are still in control. You go to the station and buy the ticket - you are in control. You open the door of the train and get in - you are in control. You choose which seat to sit on - you are in control. The train driver moves out of the station and at this point you are no longer in control.

Once you have opened the door to the occult realms and invited them into your life, you are no longer in control of them but rather they are in control of you.

We should also underline that even being involved with the 'con artist' can bring us under superstition which is itself a breeding ground for many negative things within our lives. Just as germs can breed in grime and therefore we clean bathrooms and kitchens regularly, so demonic activity can breed within superstition and we need to clean it out.

If it's Supernatural it must be Good

Many feel that if something is deemed as supernatural, and it works, we must accept it. That would be fine if everything we see and hear was genuinely good but unfortunately today we have this 'demonic realm', these counterfeit supernatural powers. To find out where they come from we must go back to the Bible and the beginning.

The very first verse of the Bible, Genesis 1:1 sets the scene for us, "In the beginning God." That is probably one of the simplest and yet most profound openings to any book you are likely to read. Literally, it means, "When the beginning began God was already there." We cannot understand that with our 'pea-like' brains, but the fact is at the beginning God, the supreme good supernatural power with a big 'S', was already there! He is not, like us, a created being.

Other verses in the Bible, such as Psalm 148:1-6, then tell us that His first creation was not the natural creation of man but the supernatural creation. He created all the heavenly beings including the angels. This creation was magnificent and it served its Master and Creator willingly, until…

One of the chief angels, Lucifer, who had a great position in the supernatural realm, (Isaiah 14:12-15 & Ezekiel 28:12-19) decided that he was not content and wanted to be equal with God. Rebellion followed, which ended in the downfall of Lucifer, who became Satan; about one-third of this supernatural creation also joined in Satan's rebellion and these today make up his army of helpers. This then is the evil supernatural realm, with a small 's'.

The Devil is not as powerful as God but he is more powerful than we, the natural creation, by ourselves. The Devil is not able to be everywhere at once, but God is. The Devil is not all-powerful, God is. However, we must never underestimate or make fun of the Devil or the power that he has. Unless we know the help of God on our side, the Devil can outwit us.

However, even for those who find it difficult to accept the Bible, the existence of these two realms, God and Satan, good and evil, is clearly shown by the world we live in and by the actions and reactions of the human race. Some affected by supernatural evil and hate, hurt and torture their fellow men, while others are affected by supernatural good and they seek to help their fellow men into a better life.

Natural Man with a Supernatural Hole

The Bible goes on to relate, in Genesis 2:7, that man was created with a supernatural part which, until the rebellion of Satan, was filled with God's supernatural power. After the rebellion, supernatural evil began to tempt natural man and the 'supernatural hole' in man could be filled with one of two supernatural sources. To whichever one of these supernatural forces we open our lives, we become like them. They begin to change our lives into their character and we begin to do the things that they want us to do.

Again, there is evidence for this, not just from the Bible, but from present day experiences too. The following stories have been summarised from coverage within the national press. In most cases, the original is on file at Reachout Trust.

> Christopher Farre became depressed and began to listen to Black or Death Metal music and as a result he became interested in witchcraft and Satanism. He became convinced that his destiny was to hurt people. He ended up being convicted of beating and stabbing his mother to death.
>
> Ian Kay who became known as the Woolworth killer branded himself as 'half devil and half man'. While awaiting trial for the murder of an employee of a Woolworth 's store he dabbled in the occult and filled his cell with satanic

symbols. He is quoted as saying that despite being given very strong medication the Devil was still stronger than all that stuff.

Joy Senior claimed that she was driven by the Devil to kill her three children. She had turned to a local church to seek the help she needed to get free but it was too late. She told the minister that her former lover had introduced her to the occult. She had asked for help and was in the process of receiving counsel when she apparently stabbed her three children before crashing her car and drowning herself in a local pond.

Three teenage boys in California formed a rock group to glorify Satan and believed that committing the ultimate sin of murder would help their music. It is alleged that they stalked a 15-year-old virgin girl, raped and killed her because they thought it would give them a 'ticket to Hell'.

27-year-old unemployed Geoffrey Adams had converted to Satanism while he was in jail. He shared a cell with a 'high priest of Satanism' and became a devil worshipper. He told a psychiatrist that he was sick of the way Christians forgave others as Satanists never forgave. He wanted to take someone out and make his mark and so it is alleged that he killed an 80-year-old woman in a frenzied attack. He then apparently set out to kill the local vicar because he wanted to punish Christians for their ability to forgive.

In 1996, the strangulation of 6-year-old Rikki shocked many in Britain. His mother was eventually acquitted of his murder but the fact that she was obsessed with Black Magic certainly led to the guilty sentence of cruelty towards Rikki if not his murder. Rikki's body was found stripped, washed and arms spread-eagled in a symmetric pattern just yards from his home. Police discovered a series of books on the occult and related subjects in the Neave house including the works of Aleister Crowley who did so much to popularise Satanism in Britain.

These stories describe actions and characteristics that are not normal reactions of love and kindness. These people were, on their own admission, affected by the supernatural evil and performed acts that showed the character of that force.

But we know Who's Who

Despite this clear evidence, there are still some who are caught up in the occult and supernatural evil realm that find it impossible to accept that they are affected by the Devil. They will say they are serving God and whatever they do, they do it for good. They might even go on to say that there is no such person as the Devil and it is all in our imagination.

Unfortunately this is not the case. The nature of the occult is to hide what it really is. 2 Corinthians 11:14-15 gives Satan the title of an 'angel of light' and goes on to show that many others, who are following Satan, will come, also disguised as angels of light, or wolves in sheep's clothing.

The art of deception is to duplicate the original so closely that it looks like the item we were expecting. Few spend hours forging £3 notes! There are those, however, who spend a lifetime forging good £5, £10, £20 and £50 notes. These fool many of us because they are the right size, colour and basic design. That is deception and that is the way of Satan. He can only counterfeit something that God is doing and will make it as near to the original as possible.

Occult Dangers Explained - *Safely*

We have a perfect example of this in the Bible, in Exodus 7:8-13. Moses and Aaron needed to go to Pharaoh, the tyrant ruler of the most powerful nation in the world at that time, Egypt. You can understand that they were a little concerned as to whether he would take any notice of these two nobodies! They therefore asked God for a sign and He gave a very powerful one. Aaron's stick, thrown on the ground, would become a snake. Surely a sign that would impress even the greatest ruler.

The time came, down the stick went and immediately turned into a writhing snake. Pharaoh, unfortunately, was not impressed at all. He called his sorcerers and wizards and the Egyptian magicians did not disappoint; using powers that came from supernatural evil, they counterfeited exactly; throwing their sticks on the ground, they were faced with a room full of snakes!

We should not be surprised, therefore, that the Devil can, to a degree, counterfeit what God is doing. Do not, therefore, allow newspaper stories such as these, send us into a tailspin! The answer is not that it's a 'load of rubbish' but that there is a counterfeiter at work.

This is the summary of Tanya Gold, after visiting three psychics; each one she rated at 8/10.

> "I enjoyed my brush with the spirit world. The clairvoyants' generalisations about my personality, fears and dreams were accurate… Their joint revelation about Egypt was extraordinary and made it hard for me to dismiss them. They were spot on about my family… I didn't see any spirits but… just because you cannot see something, it doesn't mean it isn't real." - *Daily Mail,* 12 August 2005.

But, how can we tell which is the counterfeit? That is the crunch question. It is easy to be fooled because Satan is a great counterfeiter. In the end, it is not whether something works outwardly or not, but rather a matter of tracing the roots back to the source of the power. Being aware of the root of the power is vital.

In Egypt it was demonstrated by the fact that while all the snakes were on the ground. Aaron's snake (rod) swallowed up all the other snakes (rods) and the magicians lost their magic rods. Do not be fooled by the outward appearance, check the root of the power.

A Wide Spectrum

As the selection of practices we will look at indicates, the occult has a wide spectrum of subjects. Some, at the lower end of the scale, may seem harmless but they could be a doorway that leads down a progressive path. Just as a drug addict might start with a seemingly non-addictive drug but end up on a hard drug, the same can happen in the occult.

There are, of course, some fakes within this occult realm and there are other dangers than just being affected by supernatural evil, as the following extract shows.

> "A highly impressionable public could be in danger from increasingly fashionable world of fortune tellers, clairvoyants, palmists or tarot card readers. A University psychologist last week warned that up to 10 per cent of the population, according to suggestibility factors, could be harmed by dabbling with the occult. Dr Geoffrey Scobie, a senior psychologist… and an Anglican clergyman, said, 'On one level the occult can become so important that it becomes addictive. The other danger is related to tarot cards and mediums where recently bereaved persons are particularly vulnerable. The bereaved are looking for contact with their dead loved ones and the

> medium sustains this pseudo-relationship which is damaging because it doesn't allow you to grieve.'" - *The Church of England Newspaper* 10 March 1995 p.4

Whatever the situation, remember Satan does not play games; if we dabble or play with areas that are his then there must be a confrontation at some point. A useful way of thinking about this is to ask the question, 'Who holds the copyright?' If Satan is the source of a practice, we cannot just 'Christianise' it. Satan holds the copyright and will demand his rights to the practice. If we dabble in what is his ground eventually he will affect us - it is his right!

Do Not Fear

All this may leave us fearful and doubtful that we can ever be free of the occult. But do not be worried, we know that you can be free, and we will deal with that in the closing section. Just for the moment we want to show that the occult is dangerous and we have indicated in outline form just why.

The next chapters will look at some of the most common practices among young people. You might consider Horoscopes or Fantasy Games harmless and think it over the top to describe them as supernaturally evil. However, we will introduce evidence, which we believe is vital for you to take into account, when making your own decision.

Group Activity

1. Using the illustration of the train, have a brain-storming session to discover what practices can affect you for supernatural good and what practices can affect you for supernatural evil. Write them down in two columns. When all the ideas are there go through them and get discussion going on why certain things should appear in

one column or the other. Use the answers that are right to reinforce the subject matter of this section. If anything is placed in the wrong column, through discussion and question show that it is wrong. Especially encourage any that have experienced any practices to share what happened to them.

2. Using a modern version of the Bible read Isaiah 14:12-15 and Ezekiel 28:12-19 and discuss what attitudes in Lucifer caused him to rebel against God. Discuss whether we will be affected by the same attitudes if we open our lives to supernatural evil.

Personal Follow-Up

Truth is the basic foundation garment of the protective armour for a Christian (Ephesians 6:14). We are surrounded by the lies of the enemy and the only effective antidote is the truth of God's Word. In these sections we want to encourage you to study certain aspects of the Word of God to strengthen you in the faith. We will outline certain passages and give you some thoughts to follow up. It is always more helpful if you find the truth yourself but if you need help in finding out the lessons from the passages noted you will discover help in the section of the book entitled Follow-Up.

To complete such exercises as this, borrow or buy a good concordance of the Bible, or a detailed Study Bible. Make sure the concordance is for the version of the Bible you are using. You might also find help from the many other study aids that are available in your local Christian bookshop and, of course, talking to your Minister.

Involvement with the occult can be a serious matter and some people find it difficult to be really free. The final section of this book will deal with that matter in detail and so, if that is your problem, it might be a good idea to view that straight away. To provide immediate help we would encourage you to study the following Scriptures. Ask the Lord to give you fresh revelation as necessary.

2 Chronicles 20

Verses 1-2 - notice the circumstances; the enemy was surrounding the Israelites and there seemed little chance humanly of being able to defeat this great multitude. Satan likes to give the same impression to us; he wants us to imagine him as a great multitude and that there is no way out.

Verse 3 - King Jehoshaphat's immediate reaction was to be afraid. Initial fear over a situation is not wrong but it is what we do with this fear that is important. Note carefully what Jehoshaphat did with his fear. Think carefully how you can do the same things with the fear of the enemy in your life and the areas in which you feel that the enemy has you surrounded.

Verse 6 - What was it that Jehoshaphat reminded himself of and shared with the people? How would this affect his view of the enemy? Can you think of other scriptures that show how people's views changed when they saw the greatness of the Lord? Consider what we need to see and what needs to be seen in a different way in our lives.

Verse 7 - What next did Jehoshaphat remember about the land? How would this have affected his view of what was happening? Does this revelation have any bearing on your life in modern-day times? Obviously God has not given us a land but what has He given us? Can the enemy take it away?

Verse 12 - Jehoshaphat, realising that he was powerless before such an army, calls upon God that he will do what man cannot. The enemy is stronger than man by himself but he is not stronger than God. We cannot defeat him by ourselves but God has already defeated him. Consider what happened between Jesus and the Devil in the three temptations in Matthew 4:1-11. Note what the enemy was trying to do and how Jesus dealt with it.

Section Two

Horoscopes

A Gallup survey in 1993 found that 25% of those questioned had consulted a fortune-teller; 20% believed everything they read in their horoscopes; and nearly 50% thought it was possible to forecast that something was going to happen.

People who are involved in astrology write horoscopes in our newspapers and magazines. We must be careful not to confuse astronomy - the study of the heavens - with astrology - the prediction of the future. God placed the stars in the heavens [See Genesis 1:14-19] and there is nothing wrong with studying God's creation or even giving names to certain groups of stars. You can discover a number of books that have been written about the Gospel in the stars. Just as Jesus used many practical illustrations and parables, there is nothing wrong with this.

The word 'astrology' comes from two Greek words, *astra* meaning star and *logos* meaning word; thus, it actually means 'the word of the stars.' Astrology is the study of the relative positions of heavenly bodies in order to predict how these will affect the behaviour of human beings. Astrologers believe that there is a direct link between the combination of these heavenly bodies at the time you were born and your behaviour and destiny while you live on the earth.

Historical Background

God's Original

Astrology claims to have its roots in Mesopotamia some 5,000 years ago. However, this is a corrupted form of astronomy used for predictions, but there was a purer form of the Zodiac that God created and indeed mentions in Job, the oldest book in the Bible; written around 2150 B.C.

> Can you bind the chains of the Pleiades, or loose the cords of Orion? Can you lead forth a constellation in its season, and guide the Bear with her satellites? Do you know the ordinances of the heavens, or fix their rule over the earth? - Job 38:31-33

The Hebrew word translated 'constellation' - only found this one time in the Old Testament - is *mazzarah* and means 'zodiac.' Many historians and scholars believe that this cosmic reference was a prophetic guide to the coming Messiah. The names of the constellations, figures and the signs of the ancient zodiac were given by God from the beginning but certain etymological meanings and roots have, with time, been lost.

The Mazzaroth or Zodiac in its original form witnessed to the everlasting Gospel of Jesus Christ that set free but did not make trivial and superstitious predictions concerning whether you should travel; predictions that bring its followers into bondage to the stars.

The outline of the message is clearly seen, moving from Virgo - the virgin to Leo - the lion (of the tribe of Judah).

Man's Corruption

It was at Babel that the corruption began:

> "The Hebrew name for the zodiac is the Mazzaroth. The ancient Hebrew names held the key to the original designations that were later corrupted at the Tower of Babel and that continue even to today." - *Cosmic Codes* - Dr Chuck Missler, p.200.

Archaeologists say that the Tower of Babel mentioned in Genesis 11, was a ziggurat; an astrological pyramid-shaped monument.

> "This earliest form of astrology was connected with the worship of the stars… The stars were consulted and viewed as having power over man because they were assumed to be gods. This… is the reason God destroyed the Tower of Babel… The infamous tower was not constructed to 'reach unto heaven' as mistakenly translated… Rather, archaeologists identify the Tower of Babel as a ziggurat or astrological tower on top of which priests could conduct the viewing and worship of the sun, moon and planets." - *Horoscopes and the Christian*, Robert A. Morey, 1981, pp. 7-8.

There is evidence of astrologers in most other major ancient civilisations, including the Egyptians, the Incas, the Greeks and the Romans. Some say that modern astrology began with Ptolemy, a Greek living around AD 150.

> "Astrology was practised only for kings and nations until Alexander the Great brought it back to Greece after his conquests. The scientific mind of the Greeks soon redesigned the art into a science that applied to everyone. The chief architect was Ptolemy… Ptolemy's zodiac of seven stars and twelve houses is still used today by the vast majority of astrologers." -*Ibid*, p.12.

Ptolemy, it appears, finalised the method of creating a horoscope using the positions of the seven stars - sun, moon, Mercury, Venus, Mars, Jupiter and Saturn - at the time of a person's birth. He also seems to have finalised the zodiac, the twelve divisions or houses of the astrological world, but this probably first came into being in Mesopotamia around 2100 BC. However, the astrological world was thrown into confusion in early 1995 by the discovery of a thirteenth constellation, Ophiuchus. Dr. Jacqueline Mitton outlined the new accurate zodiac in the six-part BBC television series on popular astronomy. *The Daily Telegraph* also reported on 20 January 1995:

> "Between 2,000 and 3,000 years ago the dates on which the sun appeared in the different constellations were worked out by apportioning one twelfth of the sky to each constellation... Unfortunately for astrologers, the constellations cover different sized areas of the sky, according to the International Astronomical Union. 'Some constellations cover much bigger areas than others,' said Dr Mitton. This means that each zodiac sign should, in reality, cover a different number of days. Worse still, in the intervening years the direction of the earth's axis has been slowly changing. This causes the seasons, and thus our calendar to shift with respect to the star's positions."

The result of this is that people who have been following their horoscopes were actually born under a different star sign and so the predictions could not be accurate.

Religious Nut?

Many young people know that if they refuse to tell their friends their birth sign, they are regarded either as lacking 'street cred' or a religious nut. Most people tell us that, 'It's only fun, it will not do any harm. No one really believes it anyway.' If this is true, why are thousands of pounds spent on buying a service that is ignored? Apart from that, is it really fun? Are you acting like a religious nut when you choose not to get involved or are you simply ensuring that you are not putting yourself at risk?

Pressure

Many famous people give astrology a sense of respectability adding pressure to those who do not want to be involved. The following quotations give evidence of this.

> "You might well dismiss astrology as a load of old twaddle, but many people believe otherwise... its principles... a potent blend of divination, magic, religion, astronomy and mathematics... the movements of the stars and the planets have been said to influence human nature, and to provide an indication of what may befall us in the future. Hitler (a Taurus) consulted an astrologer and so did Indria Gandhi (Scorpio) and Nancy Reagan (Cancer) on behalf of her husband. Ronald (Aquarius)... John Major (Aries) had his chart drawn up by his biographer Nesta Wyn-Ellis, who also happens to be an astrologer." - *The Independent on Sunday*, 3 December 1995.
> "There is no shortage of celebrities willing to ask for spiritual help... Jennifer Lopez turned to her personal fortune-teller... after splitting up with [her] fiancé... Coldplay signer Chris Martin consults... regularly on matters of the heart... Britney Spears was warned about the break-up of her relationship... weeks before he dumped her in March 2002..." - *Daily Express,* 15 March 2005, p.35.

Further pressure can be brought by astrology classes being advertised in education prospectuses. Interestingly, Reachout

Occult Dangers Explained - *Safely*

Trust received the following letter from one school in a north of England education authority,

> Thank you for your letter expressing your concern about setting up of astrology classes at xxx School. As the paper reported we had arranged for only one session to be held to enable us to assess the situation. Following this initial meeting it has been decided that no further classes will be held at the school. I hope you find this information reassuring.

Business too is using Astrology

> "Rebecca Nolan... has been promoting her quarterly newsletter... to UK investors for £259 a year or £89 an issue. This might seem expensive... But a mailshot claims this is 'peanuts compared with the profit you could make on your very first trade'. Nolan is one of a growing band of astro-economists who are using the stars to forecast movements in the financial markets... Christeen Skinner specialises in predicting the future for particular companies rather than general market trends. She is currently analysing the prospects of Cuba for two commodities clients." - *The Observer*, 31 March 1996.

Probably above everything else television has made it the acceptable practice that it is:

> "BBC1's National Lottery Live... Two spangly-costumed women, Anthea Turner and Mystic Meg... playing hostess, singing and dancing, and mystical divination... Margaret (Meg) Lake... in 1986, on her debut... described herself as a mix of English, Welsh Romany and Russian... The likes of Terry Wogan and

Bob Monkhouse provide droll testimonials. David Frost regularly quotes her 'messages from beyond the grave' on his breakfast TV show... Since the lottery began last November, the improbable oracle has become as much part of national folklore as Gazza or Cilla... Most weeks on the TV lottery draw, happy winners show up to confirm her clairvoyance... But as each scattergun spiel contains a dozen separate predictions, it must be doubtful whether her overall performance is better than random." - *The Guardian*, 16 October 1995.

Demonic?

This all may be true but just because something is popular it does not mean that it is evil! Nevertheless, what popularity often does, is stop us checking carefully into the subject. Where then is the proof that it is demonic, part of this supernaturally evil realm?

Whereas we do not believe that everyone who reads a horoscope is 'demon possessed', astrology claims to give supernatural answers. The stars that God placed in the heavens, for signs and seasons, have been given supernatural powers to lead and guide our lives. The question is where does this supernatural power come from; the natural stars themselves or something beyond?

If it were from God then we would expect the Bible to speak positively about it; but the opposite is true:

> You are wearied with many counsels; Let now your astrologers, those who prophesy by the stars, those who predict by the new moons, stand up and save you from what will come upon you. Behold, they have become like stubble, fire burns them; they cannot deliver themselves from the power of the flame. - Isaiah 47:12-13.

> Daniel answered before the king and said, "As for the mystery about which the king has inquired, neither wise men, conjurers, magicians, nor diviners are able to declare it to the king. However there is a God in heaven Who reveals mysteries, and He has made known. - Daniel 2:27, 28.

God is not the supernatural power behind astrology but rather it is the supernatural evil power that is behind the predictions of the stars.

Some argue that the Bible encourages astrology, often quoting the Magi who were inspired to seek Jesus by studying the stars. Here we must remember the distinction between astronomy and astrology. God has nothing against astronomy because that is studying His creation. The Magi were probably descendants of the ancient priesthood of the Medes and would have had great understanding in a number of fields. One of these, astronomy, would have helped them to notice the sign in the heavens. They did not interpret the future but realised that there was a sign in the heaven, the very reason that God placed the stars there (Genesis 1:14).

It is clear, from the events, that they were not followers of modern-day astrology - seeking to get a message from the stars. Note (Matthew 2:1-6) that when they got to Herod and asked where the new king was, the wise men used the Scriptures they had at the time - the Tanach or Old Testament - to tell them where Jesus was to be born.

Different Types of Horoscopes

Newspaper Style

This is the type found in most national newspapers and magazines. Some will not be 'supernatural' at all. Many will differ from one another because the astrologers 'interpret' the stars in a different way. The majority of people that read these claim they do not take them seriously.

Even if all this is true, two things can happen. First, subconsciously a person can change their lifestyle to match the predictions. Second, it can give a person the desire to get deeper involved with the evil supernatural.

More Detailed

The next step along the road for most people is to obtain a more detailed prediction using their birth sign. This step often will bring them into contact with someone who does have a 'supernatural' gift, which, as we have already indicated, is not from the God the evangelical Christians believe in. Scripture mentions a person just like this in Acts 16.

> It happened that as we were going to the place of prayer, a slave-girl having a spirit of divination met us, who was bringing her masters much profit by fortune-telling. - Acts 16:16

The 'success' and popularity of this particular person was because of a 'spirit of divination', a demonic spirit. When Paul cast out this spirit, as recorded a little later on in the chapter, the girl lost her 'gift'.

Personalised

An individual receives a personalised prediction from their date and place of birth. It is normal for people who get this far to check their horoscope before taking any major decision.

Some receive 'Reader's Digest' type offers through the post from astrologers such as this, one example from many:

> "I was charting the stars for a Hollywood celebrity who shares YOUR BIRTHDAY... well, YOU Mr xxx are about to enter that rare and wonderful period called the 'Golden Wave' of your life."

Occult Dangers Explained - *Safely*

The letter goes on to say that the recipient is passing into a really lucky time of their life and they must register now. Many will be taken in by this and will unwittingly get involved in specific astrological predictions.

Fakes?

Within this field there certainly are fakes, as the following article shows.

> "A woman is consulting an astrologer. He stares at a chart covered with alchemical symbols amid talks in a soothing, friendly voice about an important relationship, travel involving a relative and so on. A rather mundane scene, enacted hundreds of times a day? Not quite. This time something thoroughly nasty 'is going on. The sequence comes from tonight's Heart of the Matter, on BBC television. What is different is that the astrologer is a self confessed fraud who believes astrology is junk. The woman is the victim of a sting, but it's a sting with an educational purpose... A recent survey found that 25 per cent of the population had consulted a fortune teller... Are they being taken for a ride?" - *The Observer* 19 February 1995, p.3.

Yet, even if the information is gained through a 'fake', once believed the person is allowing superstition to rule in their lives and even this can be dangerous.

An article that appeared in the *Daily Mail*, 11 September 1996, showed how three different women could not get through the day without input from the supernatural.

> "Christine Curran's husband Peter, a warder at top security Whitemoor Prison in

Cambridgeshire, has been missing since May 14 last year. Married for 12 years, Christine, 41, now lives near Bournemouth with her daughters Hazel, 10, and Emma, eight. She is using spiritualist mediums in a bid to find out what happened to her husband... Cassandra Eason, 48, lives on the Isle of Wight with her five children while her husband John, 46, divides his time between there and his job in London. Cassandra uses the tarot cards to make major decisions... Lesley Morris, 36, lives in Egham, Surrey, with her son James, 15, and teaches drawing at Spelthorne College. She makes decisions based on a combination of astrology and the runes, a prophetic alphabet dating back to 2000BC."

Other Matters

There are other matters to consider, not only the danger of opening to supernatural evil, which indicate that we should not rely on astrology. For instance, there is the simple fact as the *Daily Telegraph*, 21 January 1996, stated that it is a load of twaddle.

Scientific?

Some claim that astrology is scientific:

"Astrology was the first science known to man and the present age is beginning to realise that it is the greatest, the parent of them all. - *A to Z Horoscope Maker and Delineator,* Llewellyn George, 1977, p.9.

Astrology claims that the positions of various heavenly bodies give information about personality, actions and choices affecting individuals. It can indeed be argued that drawing such charts is a science; take, for instance, the mathematical calculations that are necessary. However, the science of drawing a chart showing where the planets were when someone was born is just the beginning. The non-scientific part of interpretation is the main work of astrology. As such, it is not scientific.

Zodiac Signs

When a chart is drawn, several factors are considered. Of primary significance are the zodiac signs showing which area the sun is in. The sign rising above the horizon, which zodiac sign each planet is in, and then the relationships between the planets - certain angles are considered favourable, others not.

What is not made clear today, though, is that things 'are not what they used to be'.

> "Today, whenever an astrologer states that you are born under a certain sign, he does not mean that you are born under that actual constellation with that particular name. Likewise, he does not mean that the sun appears to be in that constellation in its apparent, annual course through the celestial zodiac. At one time the latter statement would have been true, but, due to the precession of the equinoxes (a very slow event, caused by the wobbling of the earth on its axis taking 25,800 years to complete its cycle), the sun no longer appears to be in the constellation bearing the same name as the astrological sign - it now is in another constellation (or at least appears to be)." - *Stars, Signs and Salvation in the Age of Aquarius*, Bjornstad & Johnson, p.14.

Interpretation

Once the chart is drawn, the interpretation of the planets showing most prominently can begin. This is based on the ancient myths and legends relating to that particular character or god. Referring to 'Jupiter' does not mean the actual planet but the legends that refer to the god Jupiter and his relationships with others. For instance, Jupiter and Venus are assumed favourable whereas Saturn and Mars are not. Similarly zodiac signs refer to a group of stars but the interpretation is based on legends that could not stand the test of time and critical inquiry! What you read this morning therefore is not what the stars are saying today but what the myths said hundreds of years ago.

Unexplained Questions

Apart from the question of where does the supernatural power come from there is also the doubt cast over the credibility of astrology by several unexplained questions. These include,

- Near the North and South Poles there are weeks when no planet is visible and for part of the year, the sun is not visible either. How can those born here have a horoscope?

- The outer planets - Neptune, Uranus and Pluto - were discovered comparatively recently. They are now included in charts but there has not been sufficient time for a scientific evaluation of their influence. How do we know their character?

- Why do identical twins often live quite dissimilar lives? Astrologers usually quote rare cases where there is remarkable similarity but the majority do not fit into this pattern.

- The light that astrologers are seeing today left the planets thousands of years ago! This means that the star is no longer in the position it is being plotted in, yet no allowance is made for this.

- Why is it that only the constellations of the Zodiac affect man, when there are other constellations of greater importance?

- The Zodiac that astrologers use today has moved an entire house (several degrees) during the last 2,000 years. Surely, this means that all calculations are false.

- Why is the hour of birth so important and not the hour of conception?

But they get it Right!

There are a small group of specific predictions, which have startling accuracy. These are used to authenticate astrology and many people are convinced by these stories. The telling of these events arouses interest in those wanting to know their future and trust in the process of interpreting their chart. Sceptics can pull some of these stories to shreds but we are forced to admit that there are some that can only be explained supernaturally. This is often accepted as a conclusion in itself but we believe there is another question that needs to be asked, what is the source of this supernatural power?

Our look at astrology has led us full circle. Scientifically we should not trust in horoscopes. Logically we should not trust in horoscopes. The only reason anyone puts their trust in their horoscope is because of its supernatural value. Yet that supernatural influence is not from God. The deeper someone delves into horoscopes the more he or she is opening up to supernatural evil and the more their lives are affected by the characteristics of this evil.

Group Activity

1. Look critically at the horoscopes from four different newspapers of the same day. Note their differences and similarities. Could it be the same supernatural force behind each one? What is that supernatural force seeking to do?

2. Using the train illustration from the introduction, define where you are in control with reading horoscopes and at what point you lose control. How can you regain control?

Personal Follow-Up

If you are addicted to horoscopes and astrology, there may be some difficulty in giving them up. It would be helpful for you to study how the Lord can help you overcome this pull in your life.

Ephesians chapter 6 verses 10-18 are very helpful. They describe how we can stand against the enemy through the armour that God has provided.

Verse 10 - How can we be strong'?

Verse 11 - Why should we put on the full armour of God? Is astrology one of these schemes?

Verse 12 - Sometimes it will be a struggle - the Lord understands that. However, the struggle is not against people but it is against the enemy that is seeking to draw you in to things that are not from God.

Verse 14 - You can stand firm and resist the enemy as you become increasingly aware of the armour that God has provided. Note each piece of armour and consider whether you know the reality of it all or whether you need to seek the Lord for further help.

Verse 14 - Truth - this is the foundation garment and truth is always the answer to a lie. What does Scripture say that Satan's relationship is to lies? What truth, that we can both proclaim and know the reality of in our lives, would be our protection here?

Verse 14 - Righteousness. Do we have any righteousness of our own? If not, where does it come from and what does it mean for us in our lives? How does this protect us?

Verse 15 - Gospel of peace. Peace with whom or what? What is this gospel and how does it bring protection into our lives? Why is this part of the armour on our feet?

Verse 16 - Shield of faith. Is faith something abstract that we have to work up or does it come out of a relationship with Christ? How did the Lord answer when the disciples asked Him to increase their faith?

Verse 17 - Helmet of salvation. What is salvation and why is it over our heads'?

Verse 17 - Word of God. Whose sword is it? Who, then, will lead us to use this sword in a correct way? Check what Scripture has to say about the natural man and his ability to understand the word of God; compare this with the work of the Holy Spirit with regard to the Word. What does a sword do? Is it always destructive? Relate this to the picture we are given that the Word is a sword.

Verse 18 - Prayer. Do we know the reality of prayer and its strength for our lives? What did the Lord say when the disciples asked Him to teach them to pray? Have we learnt these lessons with regard to overcoming those things in our lives not of God?

It will also be helpful for you to discover how the Lord has the future in His hands and we do not need the creation to be able to tell the future but we need the Creator.

Use a concordance to find out how many verses you can discover that talk about the greatness of God. Also, take time to study some other passages such as Proverbs 3:5-6 and Isaiah 55:6-13.

What do these tell us about trust for the future? Compare these with some of the verses recorded earlier in the chapter that deal with using astrology as a guide to the future.

HARRY POTTER

Background

The release of every new book and film proves that 'Pottermania' is as strong as ever. Each new offering outsells and outshines the previous one. It holds the record of being the first film ever to take £5 million on its first day and the books to date have sold over 200 million copies.

The sixth and penultimate book, *Harry Potter and the Half-Blood Prince* was released mid 2005; the previous five books, in chronological order, are entitled *Harry Potter and the Philosopher's Stone* (*Harry Potter and the Sorcerer's Stone* in the USA), *Harry Potter and the Chamber of Secrets, Harry Potter and the Prisoner of Azkaban, Harry Potter and the Goblet of Fire*, and *Harry Potter and the Order of the Phoenix.*

The Half-Blood Prince, dealing with Harry's sixth year at Hogwarts wizard school, has broken Potter's own record for the number of pre-ordered books. Around 2 million copies were sold in Britain on its first day. Initial reactions appear to show that most feel this is better than previous books. The Telegraph online said:

> "The consensus was that the latest offering from Rowling is a vast improvement on the two preceding books. The overall tone is darker and more mature: Harry Potter is now 16 and preparing for adulthood."

History

The books themselves concern the rise to fame of a very unlikely, bespectacled hero Harry Potter. Because of the events that killed his parents Harry now lives with his only surviving relatives a 'muggle' family. The official definition of 'muggle' is, "a non-magical people". Harry's aunt and uncle Vernon and Petunia and his spoilt cousin Dudley, hate him and seek to make his life as miserable as possible, even forcing him to sleep under the stairs.

Through Rubeus Hagrid, (half human and half giant) the caretaker of Hogwarts school of witchcraft and wizardry, Harry discovers the awful truth that he is in fact a powerful wizard and that his parents were killed by the evil Voldemort, a being so awesome that even the witches and wizards dare not utter his name, referring to him as 'You know who' or 'The one who shall not be named'.

Voldemort had gone to the Potters home and killed James and Lily while they were attempting to protect Harry, their son. When Voldemort turned the curse, that had killed so many witches and wizards, on Harry Potter, it rebounded, ripping him from his body. With his powers gone, barely alive, he fled.

Harry's adventures begin when he starts to attend the school and becomes a close friend of two other young magicians, Hermione Granger and Ron Weasley. They have enemies at the school in the way of Draco Malfoy and his cronies. The books are totally filled with supernatural happenings, flying broomsticks and potions, but it is also claimed that the books are also about other themes such as 'good and evil', bravery, friendship, adolescence, ambition and loyalty.

The Books

The Goblet of Fire published in 2000 concerns Harry's fourth year at Hogwarts. The Ministry of Magic reopens an old tournament called the 'International Triwizard Tournament' in which three wizard champions, chosen by the Goblet of Fire compete together. The rules are that each champ must be seventeen years old, but the 'Goblet of Fire' chooses the fourteen-year-old Harry, and its decision is irrevocable. This places Harry's life in danger. At the same time, Harry's famous red scar has been troubling him; he has also been having nightmares about Voldemort, which means a further encounter with his evil foe is in the offing.

At the time of publishing this book the latest Potter volume released is the sixth one - The *Half-Blood Prince.* This been hailed as a success by Chancellor Gordon Brown who is reported as saying that J K Rowling had "done more for literacy around the world than any single human being".

However, there are also some notable critics such as Pope Benedict XVI who expressed concerns in a letter to Roman Catholic sociologist Gabriele Kuby:

> "It is good that you are throwing light on Harry Potter, because these are subtle seductions that work imperceptibly, and because of that deeply, and erode Christianity in the soul before it can even grow properly."

We can easily be drawn into the argument of who is right, but the answer is probably both, because they are arguing from different perspectives. As far as success is concerned, the facts speak for themselves. The Pope, however, was not seeking to deal with success but a more important issue - the spiritual implications to the lives of the avid fans. This is the aspect that all Christians should be concerned about.

Harry is revealed in the latest book as "The Chosen One" to destroy the evil wizard Voldemort, he who shall not be named, whose background is also revealed in some detail. At the beginning of the series, Harry's parents had been killed by Voldemort while they were attempting to protect Harry. When Voldemort turned the 'killer' curse on Harry, it rebounded, ripping him from his body and barely alive, he fled.

Setting the scene for the final book

Some highlights from the latest book, without giving the entire plot away, are that 'The Half-blood Prince' left his old potions book at the school, from years before, and this is given to Harry. We discover towards the end the identity of this Prince - Severus Snape who turns out to actually be a 'baddie' and kills….. (I will not reveal that here!)

The potion book enables Harry to create exotic (exotic means alien or foreign – how about "extraordinary" or "special"?) spells - including reaping revenge by killing his enemies. This causes problems with Hermione because not only is he now better than her at potions, but she is angry that he is doing it by cheating. All the young teenagers, Ron, Harry, Hermione and Ginny are involved in various 'love matches' that cause the normal jealousy and teenage arguments.

We are also reminded in this latest book that Voldemort, "was less than spirit and less than the meanest ghost but still alive"! We also discover that by a supreme act of evil - committing murder - he has managed to split his soul into seven parts and placed each within a 'Horcrux'. The plot of the final book has been set up for a classic showdown, as Harry tries to discover each Horcrux and destroy it, thus triumphing over Voldemort.

Only use the Truth

One of the problems we have found in talking about this subject is the excess in the statements that some people have made. Once a false or severely exaggerated statement is made then credibility is lost and even that which is true is ignored. This statement of not exaggerating the truth and not making statements that are not backed up with hard facts is an important one to learn when dealing with occultic issues.

Let's deal with some of these 'extreme' statements that will always detract from the more reasonable and important arguments.

Statement 1. J.K.Rowling is a witch and has written these books deliberately to draw people into witchcraft.

In all the years we have been looking at these issues we have never found any evidence to back up the above claim. It is a wild slanderous assertion that we do not want to be associated with. There is no question that Rowling or her team have researched well into witchcraft and understand it but nowhere do we find any deliberate seeking to bring children into witchcraft. Rowling has found a story line and subject that many are interested in and has produced some well written books about it.

Statement 2. Most who read these books become demonised and end up in witchcraft.

Again there is no evidence whatsoever for this. I do believe it has increased the interest in magic and spells, etc. It has also probably led some to look further into the subject, wanting the power that Harry has. However, there is not a demon on every page and many read the books as simply another novel with an interesting plot.

The one thing I would like to add here, though, is that what it might do is stop people looking at evangelical Christianity. Not because the books teach anti-Christian themes but simply the subject matter is occult, magic and witchcraft, and that is what people would be thinking about not Christianity.

Statement 3. There is no danger whatsoever with these books and all Christian parents should let their children read them without any interference.

Occult Dangers Explained - *Safely*

This is a statement made by a number of well-known evangelical Christian leaders and expanded on in a number of books that want to show Biblical themes in Harry Potter. My problem here is that this is going to the 'other extreme'. The subject matter of Harry Potter is Witchcraft, nobody denies that. Most that read the Bible with an evangelical persuasion would see that clearly God says that Witchcraft is not of Him and that many were turned away from Him by following Witchcraft. Herein is the heart of it - if I accept these books without any qualifications and indeed encourage children to read them, then I am encouraging my children to read something that God says is not good or helpful in coming to know Him.

Am I saying we should not read the books? I think that is for each family to decide before God - here I simply want to show why I believe this third statement is extreme and we do not agree with it.

Concerns

These books are so popular that it seems churlish to criticise them. However, we do feel there are issues here that need to be mentioned. We should not just put our heads in the sand and ignore possible danger signs like "Quick Sand" just above you.

There has been an increase in the number of books and programmes that use the theme of witchcraft and magic. Probably because they are sold in such volumes, Potter books have especially caused concern among Christian teachers and parents in Britain. One of the major issues is whether or not these books should be placed on school reading lists and in school libraries.

These books have been challenged in at least 13 states of America. One school in Michigan has banned the reading of them aloud and requires parental permission to use them for book reports. The books have also been challenged from schools in New Zealand, Canada and England. Headmistress

Carol Rookwood banned the books from the library of St Mary's Church of England School in Chatham, Kent. Also, Holt Primary, in Skellingthorpe, Lincs, abandoned plans for a Harry Potter Day, to commemorate the latest book release, because of parental pressure.

The stories are not true; but anyone longing for the reality of such power would certainly not investigate the source in their local church. If a Sunday school teacher encouraged their children to study witchcraft, I would hope they would soon be reprimanded. But isn't that what is happening? The Potter books are all about witchcraft, pure and simple.

Whereas these books are not meant to be a spiritual treatise, they do deal with spiritual areas such as the supernatural and death. It seems to me, therefore, that any Christian, who holds up the way these themes are handled to the light of Scripture, must become concerned. We surely cannot be comfortable with the portrayal of supernatural only affecting us in this life, and that death is the end of everything. This is not a helpful picture to the reader.

Three Issues

Christian groups who are actively involved in these issues feel that there are three major problems with the books.

First, it is felt that the books are misleading. Freedom Village USA Ministries state that :

> "To suggest to any child...that there is a way to escape the unhappy, real life world they live in and to retreat into a mystical fantasy world to find happiness is totally irresponsible and deceitful."

In other words, there is a real concern that young people will follow-up on this message and become actively involved in the occult to find refuge and spiritual satisfaction. Probably, too, because of being so emotionally involved with the characters, they would not stop to ask, "Is there another and, indeed, better way?"

That this actually does happen and it is not just the figment of a Christian's imagination, is clear from a remark that J. K. Rowling made in an interview with Newsweek's Malcolm Jones,

> "I get letters from children addressed to Professor Dumbledore (headmaster at Hogwarts School of Witchcraft and Wizardry, the book's setting), and it's not a joke, begging to be let into Hogwarts, and some of them are really sad. Because they want it to be true so badly they've convinced themselves it's true". - The Return of Harry Potter!, *Newsweek*, July 1, 2000, page 4

Indeed, according to an article in the *Daily Mirror* in August 2005, there is a real-life 'Hogwarts' School in Austria.

> "Students at the college in the mountains of Klagenfurt... take a six-part course in 'all things related to witchcraft and wizardry'. And they can later prepare potions, make talismans and perform rituals. Headmaster and grand wizard 'Dakaneth' - also known as Andreas Starchel - who founded the school seven years ago said applications are soaring."

Second, the books contain pagan and anti-biblical philosophy. One example is the continual involvement of dead people in the world of the living. In 'The Half-Blood Prince,' 'Inferi', dead bodies, are given some form of animation and attack Harry.

From the evangelical Christian's point of view, contacting the dead does not sit comfortably with Scripture.

46

Where does the message actually come from? Do I have any proof that this is really the dead person speaking? Could it not be some supernatural evil power that is masquerading as the person to seek to lead me into a wrong path? Interestingly, in the real world, just about every message is, "everything is okay", "don't worry about me." Such messages, of course, bring a feeling that I need not do anything in this life concerning the future one after death. Could this be a dangerous lie?

Third, these books simply state that power is there, but no source is ever really discussed, and I wonder what conclusions readers might draw from this. In 'The Philosopher's (Sorcerer's) Stone,' Harry is told that there is no good and evil, only power. This also does not square up with evangelical Biblical truth. We indeed discover that the wands of the 'good' wizard Harry and the 'bad' wizard Voldemort both have a feather coming from the same source - one source of power that can be manipulated either for 'good' or for evil.

This leads to the position at the end of 'The Half-Blood Prince' where, as one reviewer put it, "the book leaves us in the classic good vs. evil battle". That is not true; the battle is between two forms of the same evil. This does not square up with evangelical Biblical truth but is more akin to Eastern philosophy, prevalent in the occult.

Defence

The books have been defended by groups such as *Muggles for Harry Potter* ('muggles' are non-magical people), saying that if we do away with Harry, we would also have to do away with Narnia, Middle Earth, Wonderland and Never Never Land.

Barry Killick writing in 'Direction,' the magazine of the Elim Church, said,

Occult Dangers Explained - *Safely*

> "J.K. Rowling is not alone in introducing us to witches and dark creatures such as her Lord Voldemort and the Dementors from Azkaban. When J. R. R. Tolkien first published his books, 'The Hobbit' and 'Lord of the Rings', there was a similar discussion among Christians. These books contain wizards like Gandalf, the evil Dark Riders, the Orcs and many other paranormal creatures. Some Christians even objected to C. S. Lewis's series of books about Narnia because there was a dark witch along with other evil creatures."

We dispute these claims.

1. Books such as Peter Pan and Alice do not teach about Witchcraft but rather are fantasy stories.

2. Books by C. S. Lewis and Tolkien deal with good overcoming evil whereas the Potter books deal with a form of 'good' witchcraft overcoming 'evil' witchcraft. However, as there is only one power, it is dangerous to get involved with it simply because you never know which way it is going to turn out. This is, of course, the opposite of the evangelical Christian gospel message.

There are instances where characters must choose between doing good or evil; however, this is different from saying that there is only one power that can be used for either good or evil.

Barry Killick concludes his article mentioned above by saying that he happily helped a member of his church burn the works of Dennis Wheatley but would not do the same to Rowling's. However, does it not glorify the same witchcraft?

Can we make such a distinction? These are vital questions that we need to answer.

Historic Events

Marcia Montenegro in an article which first appeared in the autumn 2000 edition of Midwest Christian Outreach, Inc Journal, entitled "Harry Potter: Sorcery or Fantasy" shows that it is not just Rowling's imagination but that she uses actual historic events that can be checked out. What this does is add more credibility to the facts concerning the sorcery and witchcraft and underscores it as being real.

"Rowling refers to Nicolas Flamel in the first Harry Potter book (103, 219) as the partner in alchemy of Albus Dumbledore, the headmaster of Hogwarts... (they) read about him as the "only known maker of the Sorcerer's Stone" which can turn metal into gold and gives immortality through producing the "Elixir of Life" (219, 220). In Harry Potter, Flamel has achieved immortality because he is 665 years old (220).

"According to Jacques Sadoul in Alchemists and Gold (G. P. Putnams' Sons: New York; 1970), Flamel was a "Fourteenth century French adept and Public Scrivener" (p. 243) and a key figure in the story of alchemy. An "adept" is a master of esoteric knowledge including occultism. Flamel is also mentioned several times in the well-known Witchcraft, Magic & Alchemy, (Grillot de Givry, Dover publications, 1971, pp. 216, 349, 352, 360, 367, 378, 384) and in a book by the editors of GNOSIS Magazine (Richard Smoley and Jay Kinney, Hidden Wisdom, A Guide to the Western Inner Traditions, New York: Penguin/Arkana, 1999, p. 184)."

Occult Dangers Explained - *Safely*

Montenegro concludes,

> "There are elements of fantasy and good story-telling in this book. At the same time, the whole story is set in an occult context with references to real occult practices and views mixed in with fantasy. The hero of the book is a wizard/witch/sorcerer whose goal is to learn how to use his powers through the occult. Much is made of the fact that the author wrote while on welfare on scraps of paper at a cafe. This makes it sound like everything is totally from her imagination. However, she did not imagine alchemy, charms, scrying, Nicolas Flamel, astrology, the Dark Side, or many of the other occult concepts and information. It is only reasonable to assume Rowling did some research... (in the) occult and magical practices."

As the above shows, it would be naive to think that the reading of these books will not generate some interest in the occult. The books are not really a representation of the new wave of paganism in the west; but they do include a great many occult themes. The books themselves can seem very 'twee' and even 'snooty', but they do not pull many punches.

Conclusions

1. We need to weigh all the evidence carefully and decide what is right for me, my family and my school. We do believe, however, that as Christians it is important to take into account the overall subject of the books. If we believe the Bible teaches that Witchcraft is wrong then this should have a clear bearing on our decision.

2. It is important that we do not feed on a diet of totally 'occult input'. Christians, especially, need good spiritual and moral input too. There may be some moral input from this series but little would clearly come through from 'The Half-Blood Prince.' Jealousy, hatred and revenge appear to be the uppermost themes.

3. Whatever our final reactions are, as Christians, and especially as Christians who interact with children, the one thing we cannot do is be the proverbial ostrich and ignore it. Searching the Internet you will find articles by Christians for and against Harry Potter. You, however, cannot rely on what is said here or in any other articles; you need to know what you think, and then be able to communicate your clear reasoning, to anyone who asks. Don't ignore these books, but please hold them up to the light of Scripture and 'toil' a little in your research and thinking, so that there is no 'trouble'.

Group Activity

1. Take a Bible Concordance and see if there are any verses that would support the fact that we should abstain from any form of evil.

2. What does God say, in the whole of the Bible, about how He feels concerning the realm of witchcraft that Harry Potter is involved in? How do you think He feels about us saying that these things are okay and we should not even give a warning about such books?

Personal Follow-Up

Read Acts 19:13-20 and then think about the following questions. Apply the answers to your life today.

1. Even though the Jewish exorcists in verse 13 were just copying what other people did and were pretending that they were Paul, were they safe from the work of the enemy?

2. Why did the demons recognise Jesus and know about Paul but were not aware of these Jewish exorcists?

3. Verses 18 and 19 refer to 'many' but not all. Do you think the 'few', who did not confess and who did not bring their books for burning, stayed delivered from their past and moved on in their new Christian Life?

4. Why did they burn their books? Would it have been the same if they had hidden them 'in the attic' or sold them and used the money?

5. Did they try to Christianise their past life in witchcraft or did they want to make a clean break with all the things that spoke of witchcraft?

OUIJA

The word 'Ouija' is made up from the French 'oui' and the German 'ja', which both translate into English as 'yes.' Personal experiences show that playing with the Ouija board can open up a doorway into occultic realms. Whereas in all types of occult practice you will find the 'fake', there is no question that many have been aware that it is 'the spirit' that moves the glass, not a human hand.

Media appearances at such times as Hallowe'en have brought me into contact with many witches. These people see nothing wrong with the tarot or the crystal ball but, almost without fail, they agree that the Ouija board is dangerous. The reason for their concern is that, 'you cannot control it' leading to the conclusion that it is 'evil'. They may not mean quite the same as Christians when they use that word, but the evidence is clear, they do not want people to get involved with the Ouija board because of the potential dangers.

Historical Background

There is evidence that early types of the Ouija board were in operation in civilisations as far apart as ancient Greece and China; the Roman Empire and Africa. However, in 1853 an innovation was created by Planchette, a French Spiritualist. He placed a pencil on castors so it could move and spell out the answer received from the 'spirits'.

The 'board' we know today is generally attributed to a man named William Fuld. Edmund Gruss in an excellent chapter on the history of the Ouija board explains it like this:

> "William Fuld of Baltimore is usually credited with the invention of the Ouija board. But if a patent establishes priority, Elijah Bond is the inventor since he first filed for a patent on May 28, 1890 (which was granted on February 10,

53

> 1891). Bond even called his invention 'the Ouija or Egyptian luck-board'... Fuld was granted a patent on July 19, 1892, for an improved version of the pointer." - The Ouija Board, Edmund Gruss, P&R Publishing, 1994 pp.13-15.

The board did not become popular until the 1920s. In the seventies, *Waddington's House of Games* marketed the board as a family game, but apparently, due to the public response, they withdrew the game from high street toyshops. However, it could still be purchased in specialist shops.

Estimates place sales of the board in America and Europe at around twenty million in the last forty years. It is estimated that seven million boards were sold in the 1970s alone, often in toyshops along with all-time favourites such as Monopoly and Ludo.

Made Popular Today

Unfortunately, advertising of the Ouija board can give a positive message, instead of a warning. In 1997, Guinness used the Ouija board as part of their Web Site celebrating 150 years of Dewar's whisky.

> Guinness is launching the virtual Ouija board on Monday as part of an Internet promotion celebrating 150 years of Dewar's whisky. The board allows net users to switch the movement of a whisky glass over to random spiritual control... Dewar was not discounting entirely the idea that the 'board' may actually make contact with the spirit world. 'Well, it's hard to say,' said a spokesman. - *The Guardian,* 8 June 1996.

Hollywood also has made at least one glamorous love story out of the use of the Ouija board. Young people can be very susceptible to both films, especially with their favourite stars, and advertising. Those who would never have thought of getting involved before now become interested.

The problem with such advertising and use is that there is no 'health warning' with it, and unfortunately the use of occult symbols in advertising can exploit the curiosity of young people.

There have been newspaper reports showing the Ouija board being used positively, for instance, to find a murder weapon, and this too can give credibility in the eyes of some:

> "A séance held by villagers has provided a vital clue in the hunt for the Kent country lane killer. A Ouija board spelt out the location of a hammer thought to have been used to bludgeon Lin Russell and her daughter Megan to death". - *The Mail on Sunday*, 15 September 1996.

However, there have also been times when it has not helped the course of justice.

> "A unique case in which a double killer won the right for a re-trial after it emerged that jurors at the first hearing dabbled with a Ouija board ended yesterday with the fresh jury convicting the man of murdering a newly wed couple... [The jurors] had been drinking at their hotel and then went to one of their rooms for coffee. The idea of a Ouija board was jokingly raised for 'a laugh'." - *The Guardian*, 17 December 1994, p.8.

We find different attitudes but if anyone looks on the Ouija board in a favourable light, find out if they have ever investigated the 'other side of the story'. Make sure they have all the facts and then let them make a reasoned decision.

Occult Dangers Explained - *Safely*

It is difficult to assess the full extent of the popularity of the Ouija Board but many young people will have had the opportunity to play with it. An average class of 14-16-year-olds asked, "Who has played with the Ouija board?," will normally produce an answer of 50% or more.

Kevin Logan records the following statistics in *Paganism and the Occult*.

> "In a recent survey of nearly 300 fourth-formers in two Lancashire schools, we found that 87% had dabbled in the occult (44% of them with Ouija boards)." pp 33-34.

More magazine, August 1996, reported on the findings of a Glasgow University survey. They estimated that as many as "1 in 10 people - 65% of them women - have been psychologically damaged by their (occult) experiences." The story goes on:

> "But possibly the most disturbing aspect of the report was the discovery of a massive increase in what's considered the most psychologically damaging and dangerous of occult practices - the Ouija board. A 1995 survey carried out by a Christian-based research group backs up the report's findings by predicting that a 'new and dangerous craze is about to grip the nation'. 'It's very difficult to come up with any firm figures as to how widespread Ouija board usage is,' admits Stuart Campbell, 'but we estimate that 40% of 15-25 year olds have, at some point, played with one. Of that figure, nearly 10% have been seriously psychologically scarred by the experience.'"

Edmund Gruss records the results (*The Ouija Board*, pp.97/98) of a survey of 1725 American high-school children. No date is given for the research but 41% had played with the Ouija board at some time. What was even more revealing was that 416 of these were reported to be 'Christian kids'. Figures, of course, can be manipulated but this is a sizeable problem whichever way you look at it. We will highlight some cases later, but one story that Gruss records is relevant here because it concerns a fifteen-year-old Lancashire girl called Ann.

> "Ann, an apparently normal, well balanced teenager was found dead in bed with a polythene bag over her head. She left a suicide note in which she stated:
> 'If it is possible for a spirit to return, I shall return. If there are no signs of ghostly disturbance within a week of my death, then the spirit of the human body is beyond human recall.' At Ann's inquest, the Lancashire coroner commented: 'It has come to my notice that there is an interest in spiritualism at this girl's school. I have been told that there has been involvement with the Ouija board, and girls are trying to contact the spirits. I hope that Ann's death will serve as a lesson for her school friends not to get involved in spiritualism - it is dangerous." - *The Ouija Board*, p.4.

How Does It Work?

The Ouija board consists of a small glass and flat board that has the letters of the alphabet printed in a circle. The words, 'yes,' 'no' and 'goodbye' are also usually present. One person then puts their forefinger on the glass and whoever is in charge of the board calls on a spirit to enter the glass.

Questions are asked and the glass moves by a force, outside the natural realm, and spells out the answer. Usually, one to six people can be present at a Ouija session although it has been known for whole classes to take part secretly at school break times.

Fear

People who have 'played' with the Ouija board will often talk of the fear it leaves. Compare this with what was said about fear in the Introduction and we have one indication as to where the power of the board is coming from.

Other effects that may take place, include a sudden change in the room temperature; strong winds blowing with no apparent source; apparitions of ghostly figures appearing and objects moving around the room. All these characteristics again are associated with supernatural evil and not supernatural God.

What is worse, are the detrimental changes that can take place in the person. Personality disorders, bizarre behaviour, nightmares, unexplained and untreatable illnesses are just some of the reported changes.

Questions Asked

Most young people playing with the board for the first time will ask questions concerning their future, especially who they will marry and when are they going to die. This last question has caused heartache and emotional turmoil to many.

God alone is the Supernatural with a big 'S', and He alone knows when we are to be born and when we are to die. Any message that we get via the Ouija board does not come from Him and therefore at best is an educated guess and at worst a direct lie. We shall see in the conclusion that one of the Devil's characteristics is to lie.

One young person was told that he would die before his next birthday and, unfortunately, this type of experience is not unusual. Imagine the fear and panic this causes in a teenager. The death did not happen but the agony and binding force of that lie caused emotional turmoil for many years.

More Than They Bargained For

In 1996, Reachout Trust received the following messages via the Internet from two girls in Ontario Canada:

> My house is being haunted by several ghosts I contacted with the Ouija and I have seen them twice. They walk down our hallway and we have pictures of them. I know their names and know confidential info on the afterlife, aliens, doomsday...
> My friend Bridget and I have contacted many ghosts through the Ouija board. Their names are Acad. Michael, Mama, Dart, Ben, Mak...
> We know more than we should do about this.

This is an example of the evil supernatural forces behind the Ouija board. What started out as a simple game turned into a nightmare that will literally haunt these girls until they are ready to deal with the basic problem. Notice the 'carrot' held out by these demonic beings of imparting confidential information that no other human being can know. The lies and deception of Satan know no bounds.

Underlining these supernatural forces at wok we received the following email in January 2006:

> Hi. I did the Ouija board three years ago and I have had the worst three years of my life. I know what the problem is through the articles I have read. Things move around the room; glasses spilt and make the shape of a dagger.

Sometimes I wake up in the middle of the night in a cold sweat and full of fear. I have had a number of scary and weird nightmares. Last year I read the story in a paper about a guy who played with the Ouija board and he fsaid some words to get rid of demons. I foolishly repeated his words and about 12 hour later I found it hard to breathe and called an ambulance to take me to hospital. I really thought I was going to die. My head is not in a good state right now and I can only just cope with the things have happened to me. I have thought about ending my own life. I have a girlfriend and two great kids but I desperately need help. Alan.

Who's There?

The above gives clear indication of the power behind the Ouija board. We may be told that it is a friend or relative speaking 'from the other side', but, in reality, it is one of the Devil's evil spirits disguising themselves as that person. The Bible is clear: there is no communication with the dead and anything that suggests that it is must be rejected.

These supernatural beings are able to pick up things about people that they can use to convince those alive that it is the dead person speaking. Why do they do it? They are trying to take control of the person and be dominant in their life. Through allowing them to speak, the hearer is giving them permission to have some foothold in their life that could lead to consequences that are more serious.

What Does the Bible Say?

Edmond C Gruss in his book, *The Ouija Board a Doorway to the Occult,* shows that the Bible has much to say about such practices as the Ouija Board.

Although the Bible does not mention the Ouija board by name, it does mention what the person playing with the Ouija board is doing - contacting the dead or contacting a spirit. As such, the Bible does show that we should not be involved in this act.

> "The condemnation of one 'who calls up the dead' ('one who consults the dead' - NIV) is all embracing, whatever the practice may be called. The terms in these passages and others dealing with the occult are frequently discussed by biblical scholars. The exact nature of some practices and the distinctions between them are not always clear. As J. Stafford Wright concludes, 'Whatever may be the precise rendering of any single passage, it is beyond doubt that the Old Testament bans any attempt to contact the departed,' as individuals or through a medium. 'This would obviously include attempts at do-it yourself mediumship with a tumbler or Ouija board.'" - *The Ouija Board a Doorway to the Occult*, p.189.

The Ouija board is used to contact someone on "the other side". This is shown to be against God.

> Do not turn to mediums or spiritists; do not seek them out to be defiled by them, I am the Lord your God. - Leviticus 19:31

> As for the person who turns to mediums and to spiritists, to play the harlot after them, I will also set My face against that person and will cut him off from among his people. - Leviticus 20:6

Occult Dangers Explained - *Safely*

> Now a man or a woman who is a
> medium or spiritist shall surely be put to
> death. They shall be stoned with stones,
> their bloodguiltiness is upon them -
> Leviticus. 20:2 7

> And Saul had removed from the land
> those who were mediums and spiritists.
> - I Samuel 28:3

Messages received that deal with events yet to happen need to be tested very carefully. In many cases, this will show that the Ouija board often lies - a clear indication that it is not from God.

> "Ouija board communications frequently turn
> out to be lies and deception. Actually,
> operators of the board can be deceived in at
> least three ways: (1) If the messages are only
> from the subconscious, the operator is
> deceived in thinking that they come from
> another source. (2) From a Christian
> perspective, if messages do not originate in
> the subconscious, their origin is demonic. (3)
> The message itself may be deceitful, designed
> to mislead the board user. English novelist G.
> K. Chesterton recalled how he played with the
> board as a youth. While he could not explain
> everything that took place he was sure of one
> thing: 'In the words that were written for us,
> there was nothing ostensibly degrading, but
> any amount that was deceiving... The only
> thing I will say with complete confidence,
> about that mystic and invisible power is that it
> tells lies.' According to Scripture, lying and
> deception are at the very heart of Satan's
> working in the world (John 8:44; 2 Cor.11:13-
> 15; 1 Tim. 4:1; Rev.12:9)." - *Ibid*, p.191.

The conclusion of Ed Gruss is also the one of the Bible.

> "When used with serious intent, the Ouija board represents a misleading path to spiritual truth. We have already amply illustrated its potential dangers to the user. Anyone not involved with devices like the Ouija board should definitely remain free of such devices for both their mental and spiritual well-being. The only supernatural experience God requires people to seek is Him (Ps.105:3, 4; Isa.8:19, 20). *Ibid*, p.194.

Experiences

Sylvia Penfold-Ivany related her experience in the *Mersey Mart*, 27 July 1995 under the headline, "Freed from Satan's hell."

> "Sylvia Penfold-Ivany's life was shattered after she innocently played with a Ouija board at the age of ten. A game with friends turned her life into a 'living nightmare' that she awoke from 30 traumatic years later after being 'exorcised' by a Liverpool priest."

The article goes on to explain that her condition baffled psychiatrists and she found no relief until the priest commanded the spirits within her to go in the name of Jesus Christ. In her search, she had looked toward spiritualism and found she had some very 'unnatural powers', but she never found any peace from all her problems that she knew stemmed back to the time she played with the Ouija board.

The article informs us that now Sylvia's desire is,

> "... to share her harrowing story of satanic possession, exorcism and the fight back to

> normality to warn others of the dark dangers of
> the occult."

This type of experience can be repeated many times as the
following letter shows. It was signed from, "Worried East 17
fans" and printed in *Live and Kicking* on 24 September 1995.

> "About two weeks ago my friend and I had a
> go on a Ouija board. At first it was fun but a
> week after we had done it, weird things started
> to happen like the window bursting open and
> the door opening and slamming shut. We're
> regretting it a lot, we can't sleep at night and
> our schoolwork is failing drastically. Please
> help!"

Sceptics would say that the girls were just imagining it but
they know that they were not. They had a supernatural
experience that was not good. As leaders of young people or,
indeed, as Christians at school we need to have some idea of
how to help such people. They are now desperate and are
turning for help; what an opportunity. Be prepared to help
such ones through the advice given in the 'Conclusion'
section.

Not everyone using the Ouija board wants to get
involved with evil. Losing someone close to us in death can
mean we are very vulnerable to the world of the occult as this
letter printed in the *Evening Echo,* 5 December 1995, shows.

> "I thought it was just a bit of a laugh when
> some girls in my school said they had a Ouija
> Board they'd started using. When they asked
> me if I wanted to try it, I thought it might work
> for me. My father died recently and I never got
> the chance to say goodbye to him, so I
> thought I might be able to talk to him this way,
> because they said it really worked. It scared
> me when I felt the glass start to move and I

> ran from the room. I haven't been back since
> but I'm wondering if I should because I miss
> my father a lot."

In such cases we need to be sensitive and not just rush in with hobnailed boots to tell them how wrong it is. We need to show the love of God and be a comfort in the situation as well, showing that dabbling in the occult would only make matters worse. These last two experiences illustrate that although the Ouija board might be the common factor, we are dealing with people and need to be sensitive to each case.

Not just young people are vulnerable to the Ouija board. *Best* magazine, 9 January 1996, told the story of 66-year-old Gordon. Gordon's wife June did not believe in getting involved in the supernatural but after she had gone to bed one night, he and his friend Ken played with the Ouija board. As they sat in amazement the glass, unguided by their hands spelt out the word B E W A R E. Two weeks later bizarre events started in Gordon's life, which would include unexplained illness and the death of his brother. Strong smells were detected in the house with no natural source. Lavender - the perfume that June's mum used to wear; Old Holborn - the tobacco that June's dad used to smoke. Finally, June had a stroke and became confined to a wheelchair. Gordon comments:

> "A Ouija board is one of the simplest ways of
> getting involved with something beyond our
> understanding... It opens the gates to all sorts
> of bad things... If anyone has got a Ouija
> board, get rid of it. It's dangerous and people
> don't understand it."

Notice that all the people that have been involved with bad experiences give the same advice - do not get involved. They realise that they have tapped into supernatural powers that they cannot handle. Most people would not take a large swig from the bottle marked 'Deadly Poison' just to find out if it's true or not. Those that have used the Ouija board clearly say 'IT IS DANGEROUS'. We do not need to play it to discover if it is true or not.

We have already mentioned the *More* magazine special report in August 1996. Within the report, they told the stories of three people who had played with the Ouija board and what happened to them. Below we retell a shortened version of two of them:

> 20-year-old Mary tells how they made their own Ouija board from Scrabble letters. When they asked the question who was trying to communicate with them the glass spelt out the words SA TA N. At this point, totally freaked out, they smashed the glass on the floor and screaming left the room. When they came back to the room in the morning it was in chaos and the cutlery had been spread on the floor in the shape of 666.

> Lucie 29 had an experience that many have had with the Ouija board. She and her boy friend Jake were playing together and they asked if they would marry. "No" came back the answer and, when further enquiries were made as to why, the glass spelt out DEATH. Can you imagine the devastation that it caused when Lucie found out she would die before her 30th birthday. This is the sort of nightmare that many have faced and even though in all the cases that I have heard of, it is not true, the fear and devastation that comes to the life is crippling.

These experiences, just some of many others we could mention, show that supernatural evil is behind the Ouija board. Take the advice of the people that have been there and do not dabble. Help your friends also to see that it is not just 'religious nuts' who say, "Do not play" but even those who were not religious before they started playing. However, through their experiences, they now know that there is a supernatural world and it is not all good.

Group Activity

1. Read the testimonies above reprinted from magazines and newspapers and discover if anything good came out of playing with the Ouija board. Write down all the things that happened and put each one under the heading of either 'good' or 'evil'. What do the results tell us about the power behind the board?

2. As leader, you are to play the part of someone who desperately wants to play with the Ouija board. The group has to persuade you that it is wrong and that the power behind the board is evil.

Follow-Up

If the Ouija board constantly draws you, it may be difficult to give up playing it. Studying the provision the Lord has made to help you overcome this pull in your life would help you. See p.35 that dealt with Ephesians 6. These Scriptures can help in every form of occult involvement. Take time to read 2 Corinthians 11, especially verses 4 and 13-15. Notice that we are warned about deception that leads us to think things are from God when in fact they are from Satan. How do you think it is possible to recognise where Satan is manifesting himself as an angel of light?

With a concordance, or other Bible aid, find all the Scriptures that refer to us 'dabbling with spirits' or similar phrase. What does this tell us about God's attitude to such things as Ouija boards?

FANTASY ROLE PLAY

Origins

In the early 1900s Jacob L. Moreno introduced 'psychodramatic techniques', which are the root of role playing and fantasy games.

The first modern fantasy game called *Greyhawk* was developed by two Americans, Gary Gygax and Dave Arneson. *Greyhawk* evolved into *Dungeons & Dragons*, which was marketed by T.S.R. Inc. This company opened in 1974 with just a $1,000 investment and became a multi-million dollar business.

Is All Fantasy Wrong?

All fantasy games are not necessarily wrong; indeed, they might be part of the growing-up process. Problems will arise, however, when it becomes an obsession and this is one of the biggest complaints we receive.

Children are often involved in fantasy games as part of their education and little harm, if any, comes from them unless the subject matter is harmful. Several years ago a children's school programme called *It's Fantastic* was shown on Central Television. In one episode children had to pretend to be the 'spirit of car crash', which fed on crashed cars. It tampered with brakes, etc., to cause a crash. Another time they were the spirit that could cause walls to tumble down. This sort of fantasy is not helpful to children and indeed the programme was cancelled after complaints. This illustrates the heart of our concern about fantasy games

Dungeons & Dragons

Dungeons & Dragons was the first major fantasy game and, as in this chapter, it is often used as an inclusive term for all fantasy games. Many other role-play games have now joined this original. We are not saying that the manufacturers deliberately want to harm children but we maintain that the subject matter of many of these games is potentially dangerous. Playing the game itself may not cause harm, but there is a thin line between fantasy and reality, and if the young person decides to step over that line there can be serious consequences.

American Psychologist, Thomas Radeki was so concerned about these games that he is reported as saying:

> "There is no doubt in my mind that the game 'Dungeons & Dragons' is causing young men to kill themselves and others."

These games are not board games such as Monopoly or Cluedo, but players make up their own characters and take on the identity of the character, acting in an appropriate way. A 'Dungeon Master' is responsible for the game and characters fight for survival with one another. The roll of a dice, which determines the strength of character of your 'player' versus another, largely governs the game. However, each player makes decisions, within the rules of the particular game, to ensure that their character is stronger than another and this is often accomplished by resorting to the realm of magic or occult created within the parameter of the game.

Even in the magic you can give your allegiance either to lawful or good gods or chaotic, those that are evil and seek to produce chaos not peace.

Violence

A concern of many professionals is the violence that can be generated by playing such games. Crimes from America reported to have some connection to *Dungeons & Dragons* along with the tragic case of the Hungerford Massacre in Britain give some evidence towards this.

It is probably impossible to prove what caused Michael Ryan to go on the killing massacre in Hungerford, Berks., but there are some clues. Although the coroner did not feel his playing the postal fantasy game was a contributory factor to the killings, what is undeniable is that he was playing the game and the reality was very much like the fantasy. Six weeks before the fateful day in August 1987 he received the instructions to, 'kill his fellow Terrans,' and his last instructions included the words,

> "When at last you awake, you are standing in
> a forest. There is a throbbing in your head, a
> madness. You know what to do..."

Surely, it is no coincidence that the murders started in the forest and almost his last words were, "It's like a bad dream."

The same will hold true for the incidents in America, as reported in the *Police Review*, April 1987. The murder of 14-year-old Kellie Poppleton and the suicide of 16-year-old Robert Ward were tragic incidents and both were involved with playing fantasy games. It is little comfort to the parents and relatives to say that only few might react like this. The brain is a complicated and finely balanced machine and we never know what will affect it even in those apparently normal.

Occult

Such violence is a terrible thing but we are dealing here with the occult. What is the evidence that playing with such games can lead someone down the harmful path of the occult?

A few years ago Reachout Trust was asked to write an article for a national Games magazine concerning the dangers. Many players just wanted to debunk the whole idea but some letters that the magazine received showed that there were those who were aware of the potential danger of the occult.

Occult Dangers Explained - *Safely*

It is not just the players that realise this connection. Phillip Bonewitz, an occultist, considered *Dungeons & Dragons* such a good introduction to the occult that he wrote a book to show players how they could move into sorcery.

Harmless

Some will argue that just pretending to be an evil character, or pretending to use black magic or pretending to cast powerful spells, is simply harmless fun. For some it will be harmless and we do not claim that everyone who has been involved in such a fantasy game is 'possessed by the devil'. The warning we want to give, though, is that the devil and his evil spirits do not play games: they play for real.

A two-year-old could be persuaded to play with a rattlesnake as a pet. The rattlesnake, however, would not look kindly on being petted and would strike out at the innocent child. In the same way, we can claim we are just playing games. The evil powers, though, behind the black magic and the spells, will not take kindly to being toyed with. An illustration of playing with the occult was found in another issue of a national Games Magazine. It said speaking, in this instance, of live role play,

> "You can belong to any two schools - but you cannot mix the black and white arts - the spells we needed were bind, unholy word, and dismiss angel."

Occult Connections

We believe that in *Dungeons and Dragons* and many other fantasy games there are several areas of occult involvement. First, there is the area of magic: casting spells, pentagrams and other forms of occult protection. Most of the spells, even in the fantasy game, need some form of verbal communication for them to be effective.

Second, we have, in some games, practice such as astral travel or astral projection. This is an occult occurrence where the spirit leaves the body and travels somewhere else. This is not something that comes from Supernatural God Who has created us a whole person.

Third, often there is contact and communication with a dead person, something clearly forbidden by Supernatural God.

Fourth, there is much involvement with demons. This includes detailed descriptions of their capabilities and powers.

As an illustration the following quotes are taken from the *Warhammer Battle Book*, Games Workshop, 1996.

> "Their... command of sorcery unparalleled... such was their knowledge that to them magic and science were as one... their gateway, the source of all their arcane power, collapsed onto the northern pole creating a region of seething energy, a wasteland saturated in magical power an open door into the dimension of daemons and gods... It made the Realm of Chaos where dwell to this day the daemons of men and other things too mind-destroying to consider." - p.65.

> "Armies of the Witch King... choose victims to sacrifice... and bathe in cauldrons of blood, renewing their dark pact with the Lord of Murder. Witch Elves eat only the flesh of sacrifices and drink blood to which they add strong poisonous herbs... On Death Night the Hag Queens bathe in blood to restore themselves... their strangely cadaverous beauty more powerful and captivating than any magic." - pp.83, 84.

Occult Dangers Explained - *Safely*

"The Realm of Chaos is inhabited by creatures formed from magical energy rather than physical matter. These gods and daemons require a magically saturated environment in which to live, and for this reason are imprisoned within the boundaries of the Realm of Chaos. They can be brought into the world by means of a spell which creates a short-lived magical field for them to inhabit... There are those amongst mankind who have been given potent gifts by the random mutating effects of Chaos. Outwardly they are normal, but within their bodies they harbour a secret power... There are men who make a binding pact with the Chaos Gods and in doing so open up a channel of energy between their own minds and the power that resides in the Realm of Chaos. By this means these Champions of Chaos hope to develop their own powers further, to become great leaders, warriors or sorcerers. Some willingly join the conquering armies of Chaos and hope to one day sit amongst the gods and rule a world of shadow and sorcery. There are many now who see the triumph of Chaos as inevitable. Amongst the cities of the Empire hidden cultists recruit new followers." - pp.95, 96.

"Throughout... history there have been Necromancers, Vampires and Liches who have called to arms great armies of Undead. There is none more powerful than Nagash, the Supreme Lord of the... Zombies are rotting corpses brought to life by foul sorceries. Their flesh hangs in strips from their bodies and their clothes are caked with blood and filth... Ghouls live amongst the dead, feeding upon corpses, sometimes attacking the living for the warm flesh that they crave." - p.107.

In the ministry of Reachout Trust, we have seen too many lives crippled through evil forces to let the subject go without a clear warning. That people are oppressed and possessed by evil spirits is, we believe, something that can be proved beyond reasonable doubt. The question that needs an answer is, "Does playing these particular fantasy games open a door to the possible fascination and eventual domination by occult realms?" We believe the facts presented above give the resounding answer: "Yes."

Should Christians Be Involved?

There are varying opinions as to whether Christians should play these fantasy games but we believe that Christians should err on the side of caution and not get involved with something that has so much to do with the occult. Besides the many Bible verses already quoted, there are others that come into play here too.

> Abstain from every form of evil - 1 Thessalonians 5.22.

The Greek word for evil here is *poneros* and Strong's Concordance tells us that this especially means:

> "... evil in **the way things can affect us or influence us** rather than in character."

Such a meaning covers the implications as well as the clear writings of the rules and handbooks to these games.

On the positive side, Paul encourages Christians in Philippi:

> Finally, brethren, whatever is true, whatever is honourable, whatever is right, whatever is pure, whatever is

> lovely, whatever is of good repute, if
> there is any excellence and if anything
> worthy of praise, let your mind dwell on
> these things. - Philippians 4.8

The following is an extract from the testimony of Vincent Thomas that was printed in the Summer 1999 *Quarterly* of Reachout Trust.

> "The danger occurs when the distinction between reality and fantasy becomes blurred. It happens far quicker and easier than you might think. Firstly, you create your character from a blank sheet of paper then slowly watch it grow into an emotional creature with the goals, dreams and attitudes that you have given it. Furthermore, you are the animator of your creation. It breathes only when you breathe, it speaks only when you speak, and it says only the words you utter. It is a part of you. Secondly, your character exists in a world that is far more fantastic than your wildest dreams. He is more confident than you are, more independent than you are, and has a life filled with excitement and adventure. He has to, otherwise there would be no incentive to play the game. This combination allows each player to explore and discover new things about themselves through the character that they play. This can bring the shy, out of themselves, and help with interpersonal communication skills. They can draw on the strong characteristics of the character they play and use them in their own personal development.
> "However, your characters are not saints, or angels. In fact there is a big drive in role-playing to play the anti-hero. You could be

learning from, and drawing on, the strong characteristics of anything from a Barbarian to a Jedi knight. The Barbarian rejoices in murder and the Jedi knight works tirelessly to hone his occult magical skills. As Christians, God should be the centremost in our lives, with Jesus as our example. That's where all the real power is to affect our lives.

"Taken to a deeper more extreme level, you may begin to aspire to your character's personality, lifestyle, and very existence. And you feel so close to it. As I wrote earlier you have created him, and fed him, until he became all that he is now. No one knows him better than you do. How hard would it be to be him instead of you? The excitement of role-playing all the time, only it's real. This is when role-playing is at its most dangerous. You can lose yourself in your character to such an extent that you forget who you really are. The problem with this is that role-playing is staged and controlled by the storyteller and, more often than not, there is a happy ending. But real life just isn't like that and by the time the fantasy comes crashing around you it's too late, and everything you were before is confused.

"The ways that role-playing can shape and change character for better or worse are hard to define. In many cases you have to have been there, and experienced it, to know what it's all about. Personally, I have had my own problems, to which my closest friends will testify. There was once a character of mine called Damien Kane. He was a vampire, with an aura, romance and power about him. He was manipulative, arrogant, selfish and angry. To him the world was his to play with, and anyone who stood in his way was about to have a bad day. At the time he was everything I wanted to be, and I began to emulate the character I played. It was only after a few of my friends told me to pack it in that I even realised I was doing it! By which time half of them hated me. I count this as having been a lucky escape.

"Finally, there is one other danger with role-playing that is not so hidden, or hard to define. It concerns the thought processes of the player. When you are engrossed in a good story you don't even stop to think about the atrocities you commit in the game. As vampires we would kill the innocent on merely a whim, drinking their blood and devouring their bodies. Deciding how to go about it was half the fun. Any imaginable action can be role-played in the theatre of the mind and yet, because it isn't real, it seems okay. The storyteller can put a lid on the exploration of certain actions, but only if he wants to. Otherwise the players are free to do anything they like without fear of reprisals. After looking into it, a family forum of the Christian Life Ministries came up with the following definition of Dungeons and Dragons.

"'… teaching on demonology, witchcraft, voodoo, murder, rape, blasphemy, suicide, assassination, insanity, sex perversion, homosexuality; prostitution, Satan worship, gambling, Jungian psychology, barbarism, cannibalism, sadism, desecration, demon-summoning, necromantics and divination.'

"Now, whilst there can be no doubt that they slightly over-reacted, you do see my point. As Christians, are these the sort of activities that we should spend time acting out in fantasy?

"Researching this article, and collating my thoughts and beliefs on the subject, has finally made me face up to them. When I started writing I was a storyteller for several role-playing games - but not any more. Now I am a Christian with a clearer conscience, and more time to spend in the real world with my God, my family and my friends. It is my belief that role-playing can be played without getting too deep, without it becoming addictive, and possibly even without the unsavoury thoughts. The only problem is that it wouldn't be any fun. Why play with fire if it isn't any fun?"

Which Games?

Below is an alphabetical list of some of the games which in our opinion contain material that is of an occult nature. We are not implying that these games deliberately set out to harm people but as Christians we should carefully consider whether or not we should be involved with them. One area of consideration would be whether these games encourage us to get involved in things that are the opposite of the things we believe in our Christian lives:

Advanced Dungeons & Dragons; Azure Dreams; Beyond the Beyond; Breath of Fire III; Call of Cthulhu; Changeling: The Dreaming; Chivalry & Sorcery; Dark realms RPG; Diablo; Dungeons & Dragons; Granstream Saga; Mage: The Ascension; Pendragon; RuneQuest; Saga Frontier; Vandal Hearts; Vampire the Masquerade; Warhammer; Werewolf: The Apocalypse; Wraith.

Group Activity

1. Arrange a debating session with the proposal, 'This house believes that many fantasy role playing games are dangerous'.

Occult Dangers Explained - *Safely*

In a debating session there are two main speakers, one for and one against the subject. They can have 5-10 minutes each. Two secondary speakers can then also take part, with 5 minutes each. After the debate is finished, there is a vote of all listening to see who has won.

2. Using a Bible and concordance, find the Scriptures that show why such practices as talking to the dead, astral projection, obsession with the occult, etc., are wrong.

Follow-Up

If you have been addicted to fantasy games up until now, you might discover it is difficult to give up playing them. Studying the provision that the Lord has made to enable you overcome this pull in your life will help you. See p.35 that dealt with Ephesians 6. These Scriptures can help in every form of occult involvement.

Fantasy Games have much to do with characteristics. Study the Scriptures found on p.127 that show the characteristics of the devil. Do you think that, if we open our lives to anything influenced by the devil, we will take on any or all of these characteristics?

TAROT

Historical Background

The simple question, "What is the Tarot?" does not have a simple answer. Jess Karlin writes on the Internet,

> "After establishing these few structural facts, we begin to encounter some more problems, which will explode in all kinds of confusing ways, in our attempt to confidently and conclusively answer the question 'what is tarot?' We will discover that the answer does not entirely reduce to 'anything you want it to be' but it often gets very close to that."

The modern-day Tarot is really two decks of cards within one, both called *arcana*, which is Latin for 'secrets'. The Major Arcana consists of 22 cards, which represent different aspects of human behaviour and character. A Minor Arcana consisting of 56 cards out of which came today's ordinary playing cards supports this. These 56 cards are divided into 4 suits of 14 cards each. The suits are normally known as Wands or Rods, Cups, Swords and Pentacles or Disks.

The cards of the Major Arcana are numbered from 0 - 21 and include, The Fool, Strength, Wheel of Fortune, Judgement, Devil and Death.

The first cards, however, were called 'Trionfi' and produced in Italy. These were later called 'Tarocco' or 'Tarok', and eventually became the French 'Tarot'. The Salem Tarot pages on the Internet tell us that:

> "The designs of the 22 cards in the Major Arcana can be traced back as far as 1440, when the first known deck appeared in Italy. The 3 decks called the 'Visconti Trumps' are generally regarded as the 'forefathers' of the

> decks that are widely available today. It is
> believed that they were originally created as a
> game for Nobles. It is not until centuries later
> that the cards re-emerged, this time as a tool
> of divination."

Today there are many different types of Tarot cards because of the influence from many different cultures and belief systems. One 'authority' on the development of the Tarot gives five approximate periods of evolution.

1. Early or Classical 1440-1550
2. Middle or Transitional 1550-1781
3. Traditional or Occult 1781-1909
4. Modern 1910 -1983
5. Post-modern 1983 -'Apocalypse'.

Significant landmarks during these periods include, in the third period, a famous occultist known as, Eliphas Levi, developing a close correlation between the Tarot and the Hebrew system of mysticism known as the Kabbalah.

> "This fuelled a new belief that the Tarot
> originated in Israel, and contained the wisdom
> of the Tree of Life. The new theory brought all
> 78 cards together as keys to the mysteries,
> but again, there were no concrete facts to
> support it. Nevertheless, something important
> was accomplished. The theory would later
> serve as proof that the symbolism of the Tarot
> crossed all boundaries. From this point
> forward, many magical and esoteric groups
> recognized the Tarot as a timeless body of
> knowledge that had significance in every
> mystical path." - Salem Tarot Pages, Internet.

In the fourth period, Arthur Edward Waite published his own Tarot cards leading to increased popularity; and from the 15th century onwards, gypsies spread the use of Tarot as they roamed across Europe.

Until around 1780, Tarot cards were not used for fortune telling but were just an unusual complex card game but today the prediction aspect has been made popular by radio, television and even the 'high IQ society', Mensa.

> Julia Azipurvs has been reading the tarot for nearly 20 years. Recently she decided to share her knowledge with fellow Mensans in Ramsbottom. She gave an introductory talk on the history of the tarot and asked what the attendees thought of it. Most were interested in how the readings worked but there were one or two sceptics. - Mensa Magazine, June 1995, p.28.

Divination

Tarot cards are simply a way of divination - the interpreting of signs in order to foretell the future. Such divination comes from the assumption that our lives or, rather, our fate is related to some predetermined events in the universe. It therefore follows that if someone can interpret the signs, omens, etc., the destiny and future of the person can be revealed before it happens. These assumptions we would say are incorrect and such thinking comes from supernatural evil, not God.

There are indications that the use of Tarot has more to do with the occult than a 'good' supernatural power. For instance, when asked how does the Tarot work, most would answer, "no one knows". In other words, people are using a power of which they do not know the origin. . This, at the very least, is irresponsible and potentially dangerous. We read on the Jess Karlin web pages,

Occult Dangers Explained - *Safely*

> "DO ritualize (at least a little bit) what you are doing - it will help you remember what is supposed to be going on. By this I mean - light candles, **evoke your favorite spirit guide.**" (bold emphasis added)

The Salem Tarot pages also tell us,

> "The Theosophical Society, the Hermetic Order of the Golden Dawn, the Rosicrucians, the Church of Light and the Builders of the Adytum (B.O.T.A.) all secured the Tarot's position in the 19th and 20th centuries. In the United States of America, the Tarot became popular and more readily available in the 1960's, when a period of exploration in spirituality began."

Means

The client will be asked by the Tarot reader to shuffle the cards and then be encouraged to speak freely. The reader will be accomplished in observation and listening, which will help the pattern and story they tell.

The cards will be laid out according to the readers' set pattern or spread, which will help them to remember in which order they were laid. The predictions concerning the future will begin as soon as the cards fall and the random sequence emerges.

As we said in the Introduction, there are some fakes. Some Tarot card readers will just be good at listening, observing and telling stories and not have any supernatural power. Although, of course, there is still danger in changing our lives according to the story. However, the real danger will come from those who do have the power of divination that comes from the evil supernatural realm. If we go to such a person we are opening our lives to that power.

Usage

Tarot readings have been popularised by certain sections of the Press. Some newspapers offer phone-in Tarot lines and others competitions surrounding the Tarot cards. As a result of this popularity, many will have regular readings in the hope of knowing the future. However, as New York entrepreneur Rita Morgan explains, it is used in other ways:

> "I consulted mediums, astrologers and psychics for years and spent thousands of dollars on it. I found it fascinating and potentially useful to glimpse into the future. I seldom made an important business decision without consulting an astrologer or clairvoyant. At the time I was a business consultant in New York, raising $2.5 million for a project... The accountant was financing my project and crucial to its success... I began to suspect he had lied to me about critical numbers. But I couldn't prove it. So I went to a clairvoyant who read the tarot to find out what deception was going on and just how serious it was. The clairvoyant mentioned names she couldn't have known in an ordinary way." - *Miracles*, date not known, p.25.

Dangers

Supernatural God has clearly shown that the sorts of practices that are part of Tarot reading are not from Him. He alone knows the future and divination is shown in Scripture to be wrong, and coming from supernatural evil [See Deuteronomy 18:10, Leviticus 19:20, and Acts 16:16ff.]

Experiences

Businesswoman Rita Morgan, mentioned above, no longer uses the Tarot as she goes on to explain within the article:

> "I decided I would learn the Tarot myself. I became good at it and read the cards for several of my friends. I thought it was harmless and provided insight not available anywhere else. But projects I was involved in just weren't being completed for one reason or another. I was depressed too. It wasn't something I talked to friends about. I suffered quietly... A theologian told me this activity is prohibited in the Bible, something I had never heard in my Christian upbringing. There is also a reference about cursing yourself by spending money on mediums... Now everything has turned around. But I paid a high price for enlightenment. I wouldn't wish the dangers of the occult on even my former accountant." - *Ibid*, pp.26-27.

Kevin Logan relates the following story in his excellent book *Paganism and the Occult*:

> "'Come on, Joanne, let's have a bit of fun!' It was an offer that schoolgirl Joanne could not refuse... the fun offered was to be another fix' for a teenager addicted to the future. The best antidote Joanne had found to those stale days was a bewitching gaze into what tomorrow held. The fun promised by Joanne's friend was a lesson on how to tell her own future at the turn of the occult picture cards. She had reached for the stars and wanted more. As time went by, even the tarot cards did not

> bring complete satisfaction, so she next tried for a penpal by advertising in a monthly occult magazine." - p.33.

Note that nothing in the end is rewarding in itself and one thing will always lead down the road to a 'deeper' and 'better' experience.

Kevin relates another experience on p.119:

> "Robert, a man in his late twenties with a long history of occult involvement, grew up in what he now knows to be one of the most haunted farmhouses in Lancashire... 'I used to see and feel things in the house, but being a child I just took it for granted... This is how my interest started. Later on, I learned about tarot cards and Ouija boards...'"

One final experience we believe proves beyond any reasonable doubt from where the power of the Tarot comes. Jim was a Satanist and was an expert card reader. At a crucial time in his life he discovered his power to read the cards deserted him. All was revealed a few days later when he discovered two Christians had moved into the flat above him and were praying to the Supernatural God. Jim lost his supernatural evil power. The story has a happy ending, though - Jim was delivered from Satanism and converted to true Christianity. On top of this, one of the women that moved into the flat is now his wife. Jim's story is told in full in *The Vilest Offender* (Reachout Trust).

Further Study

The Tarot - Reachout Trust (Factsheet)

Group Activity

1. Discuss in small groups Jim's testimony mentioned above. Where did his power come from in the first place and how did he lose his power? How can we be sure this is true?

2. With a concordance look up references to divination. What does the original Hebrew word mean?

For this type of exercise the leader may have to give some instruction as how to use a concordance.

Follow-Up

If you have regularly had readings from the Tarot cards, you may have some difficulty in giving this up. It would be helpful for you to study what provision the Lord has made to help you overcome this pull within your life. See p.35 that dealt with Ephesians 6. These Scriptures can help in every form of occult involvement.

Take a concordance or other bible study aid and check the original words in Deuteronomy 18:9-14; see also p.135. Do these areas cover all occult practices today? Can you think of any that do not come into this list? Has God changed His mind about such practices in modern-day?

Why did God tell them not to be involved with these practices? What would and would not happen if they disobeyed?

WITCHCRAFT

Definition

Witchcraft is one of those terms that's used of a spectrum of beliefs. It is often wrongly thought that everyone who uses the term witchcraft is into 'Black Magic' or Satanism. There is a major difference between what is commonly called 'white witchcraft' or Wicca and 'black witchcraft' or Satanism.

We need to understand what these people believe and not accuse them of horrific acts that are unfounded. There are a small minority of cases where horrific things are reported, such as the following article, from the *Online Telegraph*, September 2005; but these only refer to a small percentage of those calling themselves witches.

> "... are accused of a Satanic paedophile ring who ritually raped 25 children, as well as performing animal sacrifices... Police say that some of those charged... have already admitted devil worship..."

In many cases Wiccans are not the 'enemy' of the church and do not attack Christians or desecrate churches. However, we will show that, even in this 'white' variety, there is the potential to open to supernatural evil and so we must sound a warning bell but we should not malign the people as well.

One problem in the past has been the apparent secrecy that has surrounded Wiccan beliefs and practices. Scott Cunningham, who has practised Wicca for over 20 years, says:

> "Until recently, the lack of public information concerning Wicca and its apparent exclusivity has caused much frustration among interested students." – *Wicca a Guide for the Solitary Practitioner*, 1988, p.xv.

Occult Dangers Explained - *Safely*

Whether there is secrecy or not, it is very important that we seek to understand what these people believe.

Historical Background

Witchcraft has many 'denominations'. Explanations are not universally accepted. Wicca is defined by many as being the old pagan religion of Britain coming from an Anglo-Saxon word meaning 'the craft of the wise'. Others say the original word meant 'wicked'. Kevin Logan describes it as follows:

> "This form of witchcraft is a religion of the earth. The worshippers prefer to be known as followers of Wicca; the wise ones who revere the natural life-force. They reject the Christian God whom they describe as 'a Father God standing outside everything and everyone'. They prefer to personify the life-force as male and female, known variously as the God and Goddess, Lord and Lady, the Horned God and the Silver Lady among others. The female is always dominant as a Mother Earth concept, making witchcraft the matriarchal religion. They still retain animism, a belief which assigns a divine spark or spirit to every material thing." - *Paganism and the Occult*, pp.86/8 7.

Wiccans regard themselves as a religion with as much right to worship their way as any Christian group. They feel their belief is appealing in today's spiritual climate.

> "Many are searching for a personally-involving religion, one which celebrates both physical and spiritual realities, in which attunement with deity is coupled with the practice of magic. Wicca is just such a religion, centring around reverence for nature as seen in the Goddess

and the God. Its spiritual roots in antiquity, acceptance of magic and mysterious nature have made it particularly appealing." – *Wicca a Guide for the Solitary Practitioner*, 1988, p.xv.

Traditionally, Wiccans do not seek overtly to recruit new members, although that seems to be changing with new technology available, such as the Internet.

It is difficult to say how many Wiccans there are in Britain today as there are no accurate records. Conservative estimates would put it at 50,000 but, when all that lean towards the belief are taken into consideration, it is probably nearer 500,000.

Development

Many historians place the modern revival of Wicca in 1949 with the publishing of a novel in Britain called, *High Magic's Aid*. The pen-name of the author was 'Scire'. The real name was Gerald Gardner [1884-1964] and with the replacing of the 1736 Witchcraft Act by the 1951 Fraudulent Medium Act, meaning witchcraft was no longer a crime, he was able to follow this with two non-fiction works in his own name, *Witchcraft Today* and *The Meaning of Witchcraft*.

Gardner did not mind being called a witch, a title very acceptable today, but not in the 1950s. He spoke openly about the 'craft' and opened a museum in the Isle of Man.

Some other main 'denominations' of witchcraft include the Alexandrian, followers of Alex Sanders heralded by the popular press as 'King of the Witches'. Sanders led a coven near Manchester and some describe his brand as more 'high church' than those who followed Gardner.

Another group is known as Dianic; followers not so much of a person but of the desire for feminism. Christopher Partridge, Professor of Contemporary Religion at University College, Chester says of this,

Occult Dangers Explained - *Safely*

"A particular focused form of the Feminist Craft is Dianic witchcraft, which was developed in the United States by the Hungarian-born witch Zsuzsanna Budapest and Morgan McFarland. While, generally speaking, Wiccans (even feminist Wiccans) worship the God and also the Goddess, Dianic covens tend to focus solely on the Goddess. Furthermore, the strong matriarchal focus of the Dianic Craft has led many covens to exclude men and restrict their worship to females only." – *Encyclopaedia of New Religions*, 2004, p.297.

Traditionally witches met in covens of 13 people. However, many groups today are fewer than this number; and there are some who follow 'Hedge Witchcraft,' who do not meet in covens at all, but work on their own

Publicity

Witches are not always happy about the publicity they get because of pre-conceived ideas others have about them; an example is the 1996 film entitled *The Craft*.

"Witchcraft organisations, including The Witches Public Awareness League in America and the Pagan Federation in Britain, are as concerned about The Craft as parents of teenagers should be. 'It promotes the image that witches drink blood which is completely untrue,' says Kelly Dugery of the Witches' Education Bureau in Salem... 'Witches don't perform curses against other people - only strictly in the area of self-defence. It didn't promote a very positive image.'" - *The Express*, Friday 1 November 1996, p.68.

We cannot stress enough how important it is for Christians to understand the basic differences between Wicca and 'Black Witchcraft'. With few exceptions, those in Wicca would believe that they never get involved with curses that could harm people. One exception was the white witch on a 'Kilroy' television programme on Witchcraft aired on 1 July 1999, who admitted that she did need to use curses.

An often-quoted claim, as in the above newspaper article, is that witchcraft has filled a void left by Christianity,

> "Michael Jordan a religious anthropologist, agrees. 'What appeals about witchcraft, not only to young people, is that it fills the vacuum created by the loss of interest in Christianity. It's the fastest-growing religion in the country,' claims Bill Pritchard, a witch."

Be aware that in some cases these claims are true. Therefore, knowing what the people believe and learning to present Christianity in a way that relates to them is very important.

Paganism

Before we look at the beliefs of those in Wicca we should mention the increase today in those who call themselves pagans. Whether this definition is referring to the same group as we have called Wiccans depends on the person using the term. In many cases it will be one of the 'denominations' we have mentioned above but there are cases where the traditions and the practices will be slightly different. A clear definition of the way the word is being used is important.

The literal definition of the word 'pagan' means 'a country dweller' or a heathen that has no particular religion. The dictionary definition is, "Anyone who does not follow one of the main, 'one-God' religions."

Pagans are usually identified with what they do not believe but many pagans today have a positive belief. Pagans seek acceptance as a religion and belief system and have made large strides in this direction.

Paganism like Christianity has many 'denominations but the worship is of 'man-made' pagan gods and not the true God of evangelical Christianity.

Ceremony

Wicca is full of ritual ceremonies seeking to release power for one act or another. In many ways Witchcraft can be summed up by the word 'power'. The individual witch wants to be at one with the power of the earth and then channel and use it. There is even 'The Law of Power.'

1. The Power shall not be used to bring harm to injure or control others. But if the need arises, the Power shall be used to protect your life or the lives of others.

2. The Power is used only as need dictates.

3. The Power can be used for your own gain, as long as by doing so you harm none.

4. It is unwise to accept money for use of the Power, for it controls its taker. Be not as those of other religions.

5. Use not the Power for prideful gain, for such cheapens the mysteries of Wicca and magic.

6. Ever remember that the Power is the sacred gift of the Goddess and God, and should never be misused or abused.

7. And this is the Law of the Power.

Although the 'goddesses and gods' are present everywhere most Wiccans would find, or create a 'sacred space', specifically for the purpose they have in mind. This is usually an enclosed space, such as a ring of stones or cave. There are many sacred shrines that Wiccans and pagans have been using for years. Sometimes they will even want to use church buildings, etc., because, it is claimed, they have been built on pagan shrines.

In some ceremonies a Wiccan Circle is created, not a physical one but one created by a special ritual. The circle or enclosure concentrates the power, the friendly energy, and at the same time keeps out hostile energy.

In their seeking to contact the various deities, and their powers, Wiccans will use a mixture of dance, music, visualization, chanting and meditation amongst other things. Books of rituals and spells can be purchased for individuals or groups to use to put them in touch with their specific deities, for whatever specific purpose they are looking for.

Wiccans would also use a number of ceremonial tools, these include: broom, wand, cauldron, athame - a knife which is not used for cutting but for directing the energy that is raised during a particular spell, pentacle.

Belief

There is no overall system of belief, with many traditions from different parts of the world; for instance, native American, aboriginal, shamanism. Most witches feel they should be free to choose their own path as they all lead in the same direction.

This means that 'experience' is more important than 'dogma'. In *Drawing Down the Moon*, written by Margot Adler, we read:

> "By creating our own divinities we create mental steps for ourselves, up which we can mount toward realizing ourselves as divine...

> The lack of dogma in the Craft, the fact that one can 'worship' the Goddess without 'believing' in Her, that one can accept the Goddess as "Muse" and the Craft as a form of ancient knowledge to be tested by experience - these are precisely the things that have caused the Craft to survive, to revive, and to be re-created in this century." - p.173.

However, there are normally some basic beliefs that most Wiccans would hold, to one degree or another, although not necessarily agreeing on every little aspect.

Living Earth

Most Wiccans would believe that the earth is our 'mother' and is a living being.

Goddesses and Gods

For most in Wicca the deity is both male and female with the majority worshipping the female. For some, this does not mean they believe in a literal god and goddess but that they are personifications of natural forces. What most would see, though, is that their worship encompasses all other types of worship of deities.

> "The concept of this power, far beyond our comprehension, has nearly been lost in Wicca because of our difficulty in relating to it. However, Wiccans link with this force through their deities. In accordance with the principles of nature, the supreme power was personified into two basic beings: the Goddess and the God. Every deity that has received worship upon this planet exists with the archetypal God and Goddess. The complex pantheons of deities which arose in many parts of the world

are simply aspects of the two. Every Goddess is resident within the concept of the Goddess; every God in the God. Wicca reveres these twin deities because of its links with nature. Since most (but certainly not all) nature is divided into gender, the deities embodying it are similarly conceived." – *Wicca a Guide for the Solitary Practitioner*, 1988, p.9.

Pantheism

The goddess or god of Wicca is not the personal God of the Bible but rather a power that is everywhere and in everything within the universe. Many would say that the first place to look for the deity is within your own heart.

Reincarnation

As with most New Age belief systems, Wiccans accept reincarnation as the way ahead. However, they do not teach that you can come back as animal, vegetable or mineral, as in eastern philosophy, but only as a human.

The purpose of reincarnation is to give time for the soul to be perfected which can never be accomplished in one lifetime. The future life is determined by what you did in this life (karma).

The body dies but the soul lives on and continues its journey towards... – well, that might be different for each Wiccan – but it would be some sort of 'nice place'.

Magic Power

As already stated, Wicca is to do with harnessing and releasing magic power. Ceremonies are geared towards 'tapping into' this power although many, when asked about the power, have no real knowledge from where it comes.

> "Magic is the practice of moving natural (though little-understood) energies to effect needed change. In Wicca, magic is used as a tool to sanctify ritual areas, to improve ourselves and the world in which we live" – Wicca a Guide for the Solitary Practitioner, 1988, p.6.

Moral Code

Most Wiccans have a simple moral code that says, "Do what you want, as long as you harm none." Known as 'The Rede', this is very similar to Alisteir Crowley's, "Do what thou wilt is the whole of the law," however they do have the rider "…harm none." Indeed, no true Wiccan would have anything to do with 'Black Magic' and even spells cast to help others without their consent is frowned upon by many.

Wiccans believe in "The Law of Cause and Effect," that is, that every act has a consequence and so whatever you do will affect you; thus, if you do something bad, it will have a negative effect on you in some way or another.

The Devil

To most in Wicca, there is no personification of evil called the Devil. The *Principles of Wiccan Belief* states,

> "We do not accept the concept of 'absolute evil,' nor do we worship any entity known as 'Satan' or 'The Devil' as defined by the Christian tradition."

Practice

The festivals of Wicca are geared mainly towards the seasons and each festival would have its own celebration and meaning. The Wiccan calendar celebrates 13 Full Moons and

8 Sabbats or 'days of power'. The names of these evenings differ depending on which tradition is followed and maybe celebrated a few days earlier or later.

2 February - **Imbolc** or **Candlemas** – celebrating the strengthening of the light

20 March - **Spring Equinox** – fertility and new life

30 April - **Beltane** or **Walpurgis** Night – a time for new projects and untried activities

20 June - **Summer Solstice** – a time of perfection but at the same time sadness as days will start getting short again

1 August - **Lughnasadh** or **Lammas** Day – time of growth and change and a time for introspection

22 September - **Autumn Equinox** – a time for reflection on the transience of life.

31 October - **Samhain** or **Hallowe'en** – originally it kept people's spirits up during the winter months

21 December - **Winter Solstice** – festival of lights and feasting.

Black Witchcraft

What we said of those in white witchcraft, not knowing they were serving the Devil and not seeking to destroy the power somebody else has, is unfortunately not necessarily the norm for those in black witchcraft.

> "The Distinction between White and Black Magic... The history of this distinction is exceedingly obscure, but there can be no question that in its main aspect it is modern,

> that is to say, insofar as it depends upon a sharp contrast between Good and Evil Spirits... Each of the occult sciences was, however, liable to that species of abuse which is technically known as Black Magic... White Ceremonial Magic is, by the terms of its definition, an attempt to communicate with good Spirits for a good, or at least an innocent, purpose. Black Magic is the attempt to communicate with Evil Spirits for an evil purpose." - *The Book of Black Magic*, A.E. Waite, 1999 (reprint), pp.27-28

Many would want to discount the existence of Black Witchcraft and believe it is all a game. However, anyone who has studied and investigated the facts would disagree with this. One book, *The Demonic Connection*, is subtitled, 'An investigation into Satanism in England and the International Black Magic Conspiracy'. Within its pages, there are enough clear facts to show the existence of Black Witchcraft in Britain today and how it is seeking to affect society. One short extract will help explain this,

> "The reversal of Christianity is Satan's Law. It is a law unto itself and a religion to which the Friends of Hate are dedicated in their apparent determination to break down British society as it exists today and, indeed, to bring about the destruction of Christian values - and of those holding them - in the broadest interpretation of its meaning... It seems likely that they are being assisted - unwittingly, perhaps - by developments in modern technology, in particular by the appropriation and distribution of real video 'nasties'... The general apathy which seems to exist everywhere today is another fertile source of the seeds of discontent, and here again frustrated young people are the ones mostly at risk." - p.152

Traditional Satanism

"Until contemporary times Satanism has had much more secretive associations than at present. In the past, the anti-religious and anti-god aspect was prevalent in all aspects of Satanism. Although this is not true of modern Satanism today, traditional Satanism still is associated with black magic and ritualism. The worship of a personal and powerful devil is central to traditional Satanism. Those involved reject Christianity, yet choose Lucifer of Scriptures as their god. The 'Occult Sourcebook' comments: 'Traditionally, Satanism has been interpreted as the worship of evil, a religion founded upon the very principles which Christianity rejects... the Christian devil becomes the Satanist's god..." - *Understanding the Occult*, J. McDowell.

A number of symbols are connected with Satanism today, among them are,

- The number 666

- The Pentacle with the point uppermost is 'White' and the point downwards is 'Black' magic.

- The Pentagram, a Pentacle in a circle represents a name that Satan has taken 'The Morning Star'. Used often in various rituals, the circle is believed to confine the power.

- The Hexagram, the six-pointed star, is also known as the Star of David. It was first used in Egypt and the Jews started using it during the Babylonian captivity. Obviously, when used by the Jews, there is no occultic connotation but when used in witchcraft it is one of the most powerful symbols.

Modern Satanism

More than anyone else modem Satanism owes its revival to Aleister Crowley, called one of the most diabolical individuals that ever lived. Crowley, born in 1875 believed he was the reincarnation of occult author Eliphas Levi. Thought to have made human sacrifices, he was often called the Beast or the Antichrist. Crowley died in 1947 after publishing his most famous book, *Magick in Theory and Practice* in 1929.

Church of Satan

The modem Church of Satan, that is not always taken seriously by others in Satanism, lists nine statements in the Satanic Bible p.25:

1. Satan represents indulgence, instead of abstinence!

2. Satan represents vital existence, instead of spiritual pipe dreams!

3. Satan represents undefiled wisdom, instead of hypocritical self deceit!

4. Satan represents kindness to those who deserve it, instead of love wasted on ingrates!

5. Satan represents vengeance, instead of turning the other cheek!

6. Satan represents responsibility to the responsible, instead of concern for psychic vampires.

7. Satan represents man as just another animal, sometimes better more often worse than those that walk on all-fours,

who, because of his divine spiritual and intellectual development, has become the most vicious animal of all.

8. Satan represents all of the so-called sins, as they lead to physical, mental or emotional gratification!

9. Satan has been the best friend the church has ever had, as he has kept it in business all these years.

It was in the Church of Satan that Chris Cranmer had his membership. Cranmer, a naval technician on the Royal Navy's frigate *Cumberland* became the first serving officer to be allowed to perform Satanic rituals on board ship.

> "Trappings of the religion include altars, candles and a model phallus. Satanists are encouraged to fulfil their sexual desires. Cranmer said: 'I can read what I want and express Satanic opinions without fear of prejudice and I will have a space provided for Satanic ritual practice. I'm not a habitual visitor to the [ritual] chamber. But to know I have the facilities to use...is indeed a comfort'... Cranmer's churchgoing mother Catherine said: 'He is a kind, sweet and good-natured son who loves his family deeply.'" - *Daily Mail,* 25 October 2004.

One wonders how points, such as 5 of the Church of Satan can produce harmony on board ship?

What Root?

In this section we have given many clues as to the root of witchcraft and although we must be clear in our distinctions of White and Black Witchcraft, the root of the power is the same.

Most arrive at the Black arts via one of the many forms of White Witchcraft. Those in white witchcraft deny the God of the Bible and so their power must come from another supernatural 'god'. As already explained, the fact that this power appears to do good is the 'angel of light' syndrome, which has an evil power as its root.

Conclusions

We will conclude this article by comparing what we have seen above about Wicca with evangelical Christianity. Is it worshipping the same 'God' or are there differences about which we need to be aware? Even though most participants are genuine in their belief, are there any potential dangers?

Where does the power come from?

Asking such a question is easy; getting a clear answer is not. In all the years I have been asking it, there has hardly ever been a decisive answer, mainly because most do not know where the power comes from.

The person who says they do not know, but it works, is being irresponsible. They are allowing a power/force to be unleashed on someone, yet do not know where it comes from, and therefore have no idea how it will act.

Another interesting answer that is given, especially if you ask what is the difference between 'white' and 'black' Witchcraft, is that there is really only one source of the power, but it can be manipulated for 'good' or for 'evil'.

This is a perfect illustration of the shortcoming of this belief, especially when compared with God's Power (the Holy Spirit). If the power can be manipulated you can never fully trust it and you will never know when it will turn on you and 'go wrong'. Compare this with God's Holy Spirit Who can be totally trusted and will always have the best interests of the people at heart, not a desire to rule and dominate.

Worshipping - Creator or creation

By very definition, in this article, we see that the Wiccan, albeit genuinely, is worshipping creation. The God of the Bible is shown to have created the very things they worship. Why should I be content with the creation when I can know the Creator?

There is an order in creation, for instance, the very cycles of the seasons that they worship, which clearly shows the hand of a Creator, and yet a Wiccan is content with the lesser.

Wiccans and pagans will often say that their religion is older than Christianity; what they actually mean is that their rituals were being celebrated before Jesus Christ came to earth. However, Christ did not come to create something completely new; He completed and fulfilled the 'old'. There is nothing before Christianity because it goes back before time began; before the earth, moon and sun that are worshipped in Wicca were formed.

If we want the oldest form of worship we need to look at the God of the Bible, not the goddess of Wicca.

The Danger

In most parts of the Western world we are still free to choose which belief we want to follow, but are there any hidden dangers in following the way of Wicca? Even if the Wiccan knows where the power comes from, they do not know where it will lead. Only a fool would set out to cross a desert without a compass, or seek to find a small hamlet in an unknown land without a map. Following a power that you do not know where it is going is just as foolish.

If it is a supernatural power then this must emanate from a supernatural entity, but can it be the God of the Bible? When you read, in the Bible, that He warns about such practices as Witchcraft, it is clear that He is not involved in such acts; this means that the supernatural power is not of God and not of that which is good, and, consequently, we are only left with one alternative, which is that it is potentially dangerous.

Finally, remember that the force can be manipulated and so allowing the force to affect you, can cause you to end up in several places, and there is no assurance of where that will be. Also, the fact that the force appears to be 'good' today gives you no assurance that it will not be 'bad' and 'dark' tomorrow.

This is the danger. There is no clear knowledge of where the power comes from or where it will lead. There is no certainty that reincarnation will lead to that 'nice place' (see separate article). However, when we look at God's Holy Spirit we find that we cannot manipulate Him; we know where we are; we know where we are going; and we can trust Him. We have security, hope and safety - none of which is found within Witchcraft.

Group Activity

1. Discuss what you understand by the terms 'white and black witchcraft'. Especially decide whether they get their supernatural power from the same place? If yes, where? If no, what are the two different sources?

2. Discuss whether the nine statements of the Church of Satan are good or bad. Find in the Bible statements that either agree with these or show the opposite to be true.

3. Debate the subject, 'We believe that Witchcraft is the oldest religion on this earth.'

Follow-Up

The constant practising of witchcraft can lead to difficulty in being set free. It would be helpful for you to study what provision the Lord has made to help you overcome this pull within your life. See p.35 that dealt with Ephesians 6. These Scriptures can help in every form of occult involvement.

Read carefully Acts 19:13-16 and then verses 18-19. What was the difference in these stories that brought the people to different conclusions? Why was one group set free from their problems but the others bound and worse at the end than they were at the beginning?

List Scriptures that show that the Devil is a real person and not just the figment of imagination of Christians.

Study the temptations of Jesus in Matthew 4 verse 1ff and decide what was the Devil's ultimate aim. Is he trying to do the same with people today?

POT-POURRI

This final section consists of four other areas that we are regularly asked about. The fact that we have not dealt with them in as much detail as other subjects does not mean they are any the less dangerous. Any doorway into the occult can be dangerous because it is not the door itself, but what it opens into, that matters.

Levitation

> "Levitation is a phenomenon of psychokinesis (PK) in which objects, people, and animals are lifted into the air without any visible physical means and float or fly about. The phenomenon has been said to have occurred in mediumship, shamanism, trances, mystical rapture, and demonic possession. Some cases of levitation appear to be spontaneous, while spiritual or magical adepts are said to be able to control it consciously." - *Themystica Web Pages.*

Having quoted this definition, we must also add that there is 'joke' levitation. The party game where the 'victim' is blindfolded and a heavy pressure is applied to their head is an example of this. When the weight is removed they have a feeling as if they are lifting off the chair they are sitting on. It is only an illusion and there is nothing dangerous in it.

There is also the 'magic trick' where it is not some occult phenomenon that makes the girl float in mid-air but as they say, 'it's all done by mirrors'. Again, there is no harm in this particular act except that it can open up the desire for experimentation.

However, there is a form of levitation that is definitely involved in the occult.

Occult Dangers Explained - *Safely*

> The witches of olden times, too, were popularly supposed to make use of some occult mode of locomotion in their nocturnal travels... As a spiritualistic phenomenon levitation of the human body became known at an early stage of the movement, being recorded in connection with the medium Gordon so early as 1851. But the most important of levitated mediums was D.D. Home. - *The Encyclopaedia of the Occult*, 1994 edition, Lewis Spence, p.250.

There are many recorded instances of Levitation, which are difficult to understand without believing there is a supernatural power involved. One such is recorded on the *Themystica Web Pages*,

> "Louis Jacolliot, a nineteenth-century French judge, travelled the East and wrote of his occult experiences. In 'Occult Sciences in India and Among the Ancients' (1884, 1971) he describes the levitation of a fakir: 'Taking an ironwood cane which I had brought from Ceylon... he then proceeded about two feet from the ground. His legs were crossed beneath him, and he made no change in his position, which was very like that of those bronze statues of Buddha... For more than twenty minutes I tried to see how (he) could thus fly in the face and eyes of all known laws of gravity... the stick gave him no visible support, and there was no apparent contact between that and his body, except through his right hand."

The conclusion that this researcher comes to is one that we would agree with:

Pot Pourri - Levitation

"Skeptics of levitation have come up with several theories as to its cause including hallucination, hypnosis, or fraud. These theories are not applicable to all incidents, however. The most likely and acceptable explanation is the Eastern theory of an existence of a force (simply, a universal force) which belongs to another, nonmaterial reality, and manifests itself in the material world."

The question that must be asked again is: Where does that force come from?

Unfortunately, not just fakirs in far-off India are practising levitation today. Our experience shows that along with Ouija boards, levitation is one of the 'crazes' in schools. I quote here, without identification, part of a letter we received at Reachout Head Office:

"It came to my attention at a local secondary school, levitation was being introduced. In one lesson a girl who is part of our congregation raised an objection about taking part. The teacher dismissed the objection, suggesting that it was harmless fun involving muscle energy and that no-one knew what made it work anyway. The child felt under pressure to take part in the lesson and she was the one who went on the chair to be lifted, and actually felt a floating sensation and something trying to push her backwards, and that that something was evil. The next day the children in the girl's class were trying levitation on their own and another child brought in a book on black magic. It is interesting to note that the children themselves made the association between levitation and black magic. The class teacher didn't take any notice thinking it all a bit of fun. The parents went to see the headmaster who at first thought it was a bit of a joke until in a very gracious way they pointed out the dangers, and to the fact that a black magic book had been introduced. At the end of the week the teacher concerned put a stop to the levitation himself because it had come to his attention that one child had gone unconscious and another needed medication after attempts at levitation outside of lessons. He feared it was getting out of hand."

This testimony among others shows the link between levitation and supernatural evil powers. The conclusions that we drew at the end of the Ouija board section apply equally as well here.

Pendulum Swinging

On the Mystical World Wide Web we read the following concerning the history of the pendulum:

"Dowsing is reported to date back approximately 7000 years but origins are still unknown. It is accepted, however, that the Egyptians used images of forked rods in some of their artwork as did the Ancient Chinese kings. In Europe, it was known for dowsing to be used in the Middle Ages to find coal deposits. Since this time people have dowsed for everything from lost objects to missing people, some of them are reported to be very accurate although the scientific community as a whole have yet to decide if they support or refute this ability. Some people earn money by advising mining companies before they carry out test drilling/core sample."

This is the type of practice that people conclude is innocent fun and there can be no connection between the needle on a bit of string and the occult.

Further investigation shows that things are not as clear as all that. For instance, one course on learning how to use the pendulum gives as an example of the benefits the ability to receive information from spirit guides. (Interlink, Kansas State, USA.) Another example is that in the history of the development of the Ouija board Gruss tells us:

> "Fourth-century Byzantine historian Ammianus Marcellinus records one of the earliest detailed accounts of divination, which used a pendulum and a dish engraved with the alphabet." - *The Ouija Board*, Edmund Gruss, p.9.

The *Encyclopaedia of the Occult* also informs us that divination is:

> "The method of obtaining knowledge of the unknown or the future by means of omens... The derivation of the word supposes a direct message from the gods to the diviner... The methods of divination are many and various, and strangely enough in their variety are confined to no one corner of the globe." - *The Encyclopaedia of the Occult*, 1994 edition, Lewis Spence, pp.125/126.

The following information is found on the *Psitronics Visions Inc* web site and again gives some interesting insights into the history and practice of the pendulum.

> "Since ancient times diviners and oracles have been highly honored for their psychic ability to predict the future. Their messages were perceived to be given by

divine inspiration… through the response of certain objects (i.e., pendulums). The renowned Greek

Oracles at Delphi maintained a strong influence over the people for centuries, even changing the direction of history... The power of divining unknown for future information is a natural ability we all have. By using an instrument or tool as an indicating device we can directly access information held in the subconscious mind... The success of divining for information is largely dependent upon three things; the skill of the seeker, the sensitivity of the tools used, and how the request is made. Divining skill is achieved by practice, patience and learning to disassociate... by using the psychic breath (focus your awareness between your eyes, take a deep breath and step backward into your head, focusing inward, letting go of the conscious mind controller as you exhale.) Usually three breaths are enough; one breath will do it when you become skilled. When your conscious mind-chatter stills, and you feel yourself expand, you are in your psychic-subconscious space."

In the light of the above, we conclude that this is not a harmless practice. At best, it is delving into our unknown psyche and allowing the swing of an object to decide major decisions in our life. At worst, we are being instructed by evil supernatural powers. Either way, it is a road to avoid because the former can bring us into the bondage of superstitions and the latter into the bondage of evil spirits.

The dowsing rod also comes into this category. Many feel it's a harmless activity and that the power to move the rod to find water, etc., is latent within man. The history of the subject does not give cause for such confidence.

Pot Pourri - Pendulum Swinging

"This ancient divining rod was a form of rhabdomancy or divination by means of little pieces of stick. In Germany it was known as the 'wishing-rod' and was used just as fortune tellers use cards, coffee or tea-grounds at the present day... As to theory for these movements... A modern scientist gives his opinion that very possibly it is due to a faculty in the 'dowser' akin to that possessed by a medium: 'some transcendental perceptive power unconsciously possessed by certain persons, a faculty analogous to what is called clairvoyance.'" - Spence, p.128.

This connection is further established by a Pendulum Divining Kit called 'the Oracle', that can be purchased over the Internet for just $49.95. The advertisement shows seven possible combinations of the same rod, and the different descriptions show clearly the connection between all forms of pendulum swinging and dowsing. Below we give a selection of these descriptions.

"Spring Pendulum. The most energy-sensitive divining device in the world today. So little movement of the arm is required, it almost operates by telekinesis. Gives direct access to the subconscious mind and the common consciousness. Uses: predict stock market; lottery; resolve relationship questions, diagnose health problems... Mini L-Rod. Handy for directional dowsing, water, maps, pipes, minerals, locating lost articles, percentages, entity detection, etc. Wand Pendulum. Highly sensitive chain pendulum for divining, dowsing, map dowsing, yes/no answers, lottery numbers, financial info, entity detection, etc."

Ghosts

How many times do we hear the question; 'Do you believe in ghosts?' Yet it is difficult to give a straightforward answer. The moment you say, 'Yes' the questioner has made up their own mind as to what you are saying and does not necessarily hear the 'but...' that follows. A very definite 'but' it is, too. I do believe in ghosts but I do not believe that they are the spirits of the dead that have not as yet found rest or as I heard once "Someone who has died but does not know it." Many say that ghosts exist but will not necessarily be clear as to what they are. For instance, there were five stories printed in the teenagers' magazine, *It's Bliss* Hallowe'en special.

> "Tamsin, 15, from Dundee believes she lives in a haunted house after she saw two ghostly nuns wandering through her garden... Sarah. 17, didn't believe in ghosts until she saw a mysterious face at the window on a trip to the Scottish Highlands... Lucy, 15, and her family from Gloucester saw an apparition - and even the police agreed it was a ghost... Sarbjit, 16, from London actually quite likes the fact that her house is haunted... Nicola, 15, from Nottingham had a real holiday from hell in a spooky old Devon farmhouse."

The experiences of these young people among others led them to believe in ghosts but they did not know exactly what they saw. We would say that from the evidence gathered over the years and from the Biblical perspective, the conclusion beyond reasonable doubt is that these are evil spirits manifesting themselves as dead people.

Over the past few years the detection and removal of ghosts has become big business. Societies such as the *Association for the Scientific Study of Anomalous Phenomena* (ASSAP) spend time and money trying to prove the existence of ghosts.

"A few years ago the average ghostbuster would come armed with little more than a crucifix, silver bullet and bag of garlic. But even the world of the paranormal is now falling prey to the march of high technology as lasers, scanners and magnetic detectors are trained on those elusive will o' the wisps and muffled screams in the wardrobe." - *The Times*, 4 September 1996.

However, millions of dollars are spent to set up other groups just to prove that all such phenomena have a rational explanation.

"Twenty years ago, a band of scientists and writers, and the magician James Randi, founded the Committee for the Scientific investigation of Claims of the Paranormal (CSICOP)." - *New Scientist*, 13 July 1996, p.47.

This Society, full of sceptics, concludes that all appearances have a rational explanation and that there is nothing there whether the 'living dead' or evil spirits. Whereas they appear to be able to explain much away, a small percentage seems to have no rational explanation and must have a supernatural background.

On a different level, Hollywood want to picture ghosts as friendly and helpful. Casper the friendly ghost became a big hit with children in 1995. If these were just friendly beings, this portrayal would not be a problem but if they are demonic beings, it is opening a doorway that could be very harmful. *The Daily Mirror* carried an article about a real life Casper and asked other children with such experiences to come forward.

Occult Dangers Explained - *Safely*

> "Schoolgirl Melissa Liversage... has her very own Casper at home. She'll be watching carefully to see if Casper has the same wicked sense of humour as her paranormal pal Spooky. 'His favourite trick is moving my Take That doll,' says the 13-year-old from Liverpool. 'He knows it's my most precious toy, and he likes to tease me.'" - Saturday 29 July 1995, p.7.

The results of these manifestations are interesting. For many there is a fear and, indeed, the ghosts apparently are evil; for others there is an acceptance and a friendship. Not all stories of ghosts are scary and some, especially children, accept them and in some cases even make friends with them.

> "Psychologist Cassandra Eason says: 'These "friendly ghosts" are far more common than adults allow themselves to think. But children are often afraid to speak about them because they sense the tear of the adults around them... I simply believe young children have much easier access to the psychic than adults. It's very common and nothing to be frightened of.'" - *Ibid.*

A *Daily Mail* reader in October 1 996 gave similar advice. The reader was responding to a letter where a worried parent wanted advice because her 'deceased mother' used to visit her son. The writer of the letter had the same experience and advised,

> "My advice to your reader is to continue to listen to what her son has to say and when he is old enough she can explain that he is psychic. I realise that many children do have overactive imaginations, but as close relatives often appear initially, as in your reader's case,

> then parents could very quickly establish whether their child is psychic from the information that the child recalls."

This advice we believe is dangerous as we will show in a moment but we should also note that it seems to be the opposite end of the spectrum from parents telling their children there are no such things as ghosts. Nevertheless, are not both extremes wrong? To tell them to make friends with the ghost is to encourage them to be involved in supernatural evil but simply telling them they do not exist is to open up problems if they should ever have such a supernatural experience.

Such advice above is potentially dangerous because of the bad experiences that people have suffered. These range from the family that had to move out of their house because of the activities of a Saxon ghost:

> "A mother of two has been re-housed because her home on a Saxon burial ground was haunted by a ghost called Antonia... Mrs Chambers had a problem with her son, who kept seeing this ghost. Antonia, by the bed... both her children had been mysteriously pushed down the stairs and her daughter had to be taken to hospital." - *Daily Telegraph*, 24 March 1995.

To the boy who committed suicide after watching the BBC programme *Ghostwatch* in October 1992. The Broadcasting Standards Council condemned the showing of the programme and ruled that:

> "Showing scratched faces of children and referring to the mutilation of a dog and a corpse were inappropriate for screening straight after the 9pm family viewing watershed... The council... also ruled that the

> BBC was wrong to build a sense of menace
> into a documentary-style programme about a
> haunting of a suburban house without giving
> adequate warning that it was a hoax." - *The
> Times*, 29 June 1995.

Whatever the case, and whether we make friends or are afraid, just who or what are we dealing with or talking to?

The Bible shows [Luke 16:26] that there is no contact between the living and the dead and that we are not to try [Deuteronomy 18:11]. Therefore, any contact that there is does not come from God's supernatural realm as He has instructed us not to do it. The only conclusion, therefore, is that the contact comes from the deceptive false world of supernatural evil. Be aware that opening yourself up to contact with ghosts is bringing you into contact with evil.

The testimony of former medium Dr Raphael Gasson illustrates this point. Gasson, in his book *The Challenging Counterfeit,* shows how he spent years convinced that he was talking to the dead, but that he had to give it all up and find deliverance when he realised that the apparently helpful spirits he contacted were, in reality, evil.

Music

All types of music can influence our lives in various ways but we must be quite clear that not all that influence is satanic. When my kids grew into teenagers, 'unusual musical strains' began to come from every room. I would have described the style as rock or hard rock but today it might be grunge, acid or any one of a vast selection of names. My first reaction was to tell them that it was satanic and turn it off but I stopped long enough to work it through.

As I thought about it, I first realised that I just did not like the music and that made it neither right nor wrong, just a matter of taste. I then realised listening to some of the words that many songs had nothing wrong with them and listening to such songs would probably not bring my kids into occult influence any more than the Mr Men songs had many years before.

There are other matters to consider such as, if they spend too much time and money on the music and not on Christian matters, they are likely to grow cold as far as the Lord is concerned. But that, of course, can happen to anyone with any habit or fad and that does not make music itself Satanic.

I have also concluded that some of the stories about backtracking are exaggerated. Backtracking is the phenomenon that when you play a record backwards, you can hear occultic or blasphemous messages. I listened to one tape full of examples and although there were one or two that seemed pretty convincing, the overwhelming majority seemed to be imagination. I even came to suspect that if you played 'Amazing Grace' backwards you would hear the same sort of messages.

What am I saying: that all rock music is okay? No, but I am warning against extremes and although there may be problems with a few groups with back-masking, etc., the main problem it seems to me is the lifestyle of the groups and the lyrics of the songs. Check out interviews in music magazines with your kids' favourite groups and see if they mention their spiritual standing, especially if it involves occultic practices. Try to work out the lyrics of the songs and see what your children are being encouraged to do.

To explain what I mean by the fact that it is not necessarily one type of music that can open up doors to the occult, we list below two very different examples. First, here is an example of the extreme demonic influence in some types of music:

> "Having produced a few unsavoury acts of our own over the years... Ossie Osbourne bit the heads off bats; Sinead O'Conner tore up the Pope's portrait... But Marilyn Manson - a title

121

Occult Dangers Explained - *Safely*

abridged from the names of movie star Marilyn Monroe and hippie cult killer Charles Manson - go beyond anything mainstream audiences are likely to have witnessed before. The group's crowd-pleasing repertoire includes torturing animals on stage, smoking dried human remains, and performing depraved sex acts to its own musical accompaniment. The band's members are devotees of the San Francisco-based Church of Satan, which believes in the ultimate triumph of evil. Their latest record Antichrist Superstar has rocketed to No. 3 in America's album charts, provoking a horrified reaction from church and community leaders. Delores Tucker, head of a Washington-based pressure group which monitors the music industry, calls Antichrist Superstar: 'The sickest, nastiest, most pornographic record ever to be targeted at this nation's children.'" - *The Express*, November 10 1996, p.79.

That is the mixture that there is in the secular rock world, but what about so-called Christian Rock'? The following would suggest that there are problems here too:

"Convictions must be based on the Word of God and not personal tastes, likes, and dislikes. Since most of religious rock, or so-called contemporary Christian music, has its roots in, and draws its inspiration from, secular rock 'n' roll, the result is worldliness in the music, and even worse, worldliness through music invading the church. Further, it authenticates the rock sound by having professing Christians playing the music. When one applies the standards of Scripture to this form of worldliness (e.g., II Cor. 6:17, I

Thes.5:21,22; Rom.12:2; I Jn.2:15,16; Js.4:4; etc.), the wrongness of such music should be obvious to all who truly desire to please their Lord. Titus 1:9 - 'Holding fast the faithful word as he hath been taught, that he may be able by sound doctrine both to exhort and to convince the gainsayers.'" - *Biblical Discernment Ministries* - Revised 1/94

If we want to reach others with contemporary music, there seem to be so many pitfalls. There are areas that we may not have thought about and things that we accept without thinking, until challenged. This can be a very emotive area but for those who want God's way let's encourage them to check out the reality of what is going on. I quote below some of the other information put out by the *Biblical Discernment Ministries.*

"Larry Norman is frequently dubbed 'the father of Christian rock'. Norman makes the incredulous statement that rock 'n' roll music originated in the Church hundreds of years ago, and that the devil stole it... in another song he refers to Christ (at His return for His Church) as an 'Unidentified Flying Object'... The origin of rock music and the term 'rock 'n' roll' are interesting ones. In the early 1950s, a disc-jockey named Alan Freed was one of the first white people to be involved in 'rhythm & blues' music, which was the direct forerunner of rock 'n' roll... Rock 'n' roll was a kind of fusion between rhythm & blues and country & western music... Freed had been receiving bizarre reports concerning kids' reactions to this new music, so decided to name it after a ghetto term that black people used for pre-marital sex in the back seat of a car - hence, the term 'rock 'n' roll' was coined. Contrast the above true account of the origin of rock'n'roll music with that told us by the so-called 'Christian' rock band Petra in the lyrics of one of their songs; i.e., that God was the source of rock 'n' roll!: God gave rock 'n' roll to you, Put it in the soul of everyone, If you love the sound, And don't forget the Source, You can turn-a-round, You can change your course. There appears to be a parallel between the attempt today to "Christianize" rock music and the "Christianization" of various pagan religious practices in fourth century Rome."

We must consider the facts and make a choice before the Lord. But just in case you feel it is only rock music I am talking about, now as they say for something completely different.

The Mediaeval Babes are a group of women who sing Latin plainsong and Gregorian chants. In October 1997 they released their single 'Salva Nos' (Save Us). Here the words are not new and are certainly not satanic but it was the girls' lifestyle that could cause problems to Christians. They felt that they wanted to take their songs into the churches and minister to Christians in a new way. However, their Web pages indicated more occultic than Godly influence and there would always be the possibility of being influenced by those forces not of God.

Group Activity

Make a list of all the activities you feel are somehow involved with the occult. How will you ensure that you will not get involved in these things while still living an enjoyable life? What sensible and logical answers do you give to someone who says these things are okay and that they are not going against God by being involved in them'?

Follow-Up

If you have found any of these practices and pastimes mentioned here a problem, it may be difficult to give it up. It would be helpful for you to study what provision the Lord has made to help you overcome this pull within your life. See p.35 that dealt with Ephesians 6. These Scriptures can help in every form of occult involvement.

To be able to know that something is counterfeit and wrong, we have to know our own gospel. Read the summary in I Corinthians 15:1-3 and if possible the whole of the Book of Romans (especially chapters 1-8). Then, using specific verses that you have read, write out several sentences that sum up the essential gospel of Jesus Christ. What in these statements would show that the many practices we have mentioned in this book are wrong? Are there any we have included that you do not think are wrong or are doorways to the occult? If so, consider how they positively agree and move towards the life that is summed up by the gospel you have written down.

Section Three

Conclusion

We have looked at several examples of occult activity and yet there are many others. At the end of each section we have concluded that the power source is supernatural evil. If you have been involved in occult activity it can be frightening and so in this section we want to help with what you can do. We also want to show how Christians can help others caught up in such situations.

Know Our Enemy

If we are not to be tricked by Satan, we need to know his schemes. Paul writing to both the Corinthian and Ephesian churches [see 2 Corinthians 2:11 and Ephesians 6:11] encourages them not to be ignorant of the Devil's schemes. Unfortunately, many seem not to be taking this advice. Some would say that we should not concentrate on the Devil. I would agree that we should not glorify the Devil and his position, but we should at least take the time to see what God has said in the Bible. If He has taken the trouble to write to us, we should at least take the time to read and digest it.

The Bible shows the following main points about Satan's character that we be aware of.

A deceiver - Revelation 12:9 - Satan pretends to be a good force and bring blessing into our lives. On the outside he appears as the 'angel of light', but scratch the surface and you find his true colours.

One who **causes doubt** in God - Genesis 3:1-5 - The first temptation Satan ever brought to mankind was to sow doubt by asking, "Did God really say that?"

A liar - John 8:44 - He cannot tell the truth without an ulterior motive. This is the exact opposite of God who cannot tell a lie. Satan, however, delights in telling half-truths that cause confusion. Alternatively the Devil will only tell the truth when it brings glory and power to him.

A tempter - Matthew 4:1 - He tempts us always to rebel against God and His ways [see Matthew 4:2ff]. Compare this with 1 Samuel 15:23 where we are told that rebellion is the seedbed of witchcraft. This is a very interesting insight to Satan's character.

A devourer - 1 Peter 5:8 - Please note it says, "If he can"! Many Christians become frightened as they read these verses, but note carefully the context, especially,

- This is a warning. God does not mock us; we can do something about it, v.9.
- Satan is like a roaring lion - lots of noise to frighten.
- Satan seeks someone to 'swallow up', 'gulp down', but not everyone is available. Sin, broken fellowship, etc., give him the chance but those walking in the true Christian Life with Jesus Christ have His protection.

Satan seeks to deceive us, tell us lies about God's security and then devour us with fear. He tries to paralyse us into a 'ghetto-like' experience. If he can keep us away from the people he is affecting then they will never be free. We need to get out of our 'ghettos' with the confidence of 1 John 4:18.

Know What a Christian is

A Christian is not just someone who goes to church. You cannot be born a Christian; you must make a decision to accept Jesus Christ as your way of life. One of the things that then happens is all the spiritual and practical salvation that Jesus obtained when He died on the Cross, becomes reality in our lives. In John 19:30 Jesus says, 'It is finished.' What is finished? Our full and complete salvation and deliverance from the power of supernatural evil that causes fear and depression. John gives us further understanding of this phrase in his first letter recorded later in the Bible.

What it means to me - 1 John 2:1-2

The truth of these verses can change our spiritual life. John first reminds us that we have an Advocate, Who is vital for us, if we are to deal with the power and guilt of sin. The Greek word for advocate is *parakletos* and it literally means, "One called alongside to help." First, therefore, we are told that Jesus is there to help us be free from our sin.

The words 'with the Father' in this verse, literally mean, 'facing the Father'. In other words, He is always in the Father's presence pleading my case and praying (interceding) for me.

Propitiation or satisfaction means that Jesus satisfies the Father over the guilt and penalty of our sin. We do not have to be punished for sin because Jesus satisfied the Father's heart and paid the penalty for us.

This is our 'mercy-seat'; the place in the Old Testament Tabernacle where God used to appear to talk to the High Priest. This is the place where we can approach the Living God, not in fear, but in trust because of our Lord Jesus Christ.

Bible scholar, Wuest, paraphrases this verse as:

> And if anyone commits an act of sin, One who pleads our cause we constantly have facing the Father, Jesus Christ the righteous One. And He Himself is a satisfaction for our sins...

Relationship to the world around - 1 John 5:4

Despite the spiritual battle that often rages around us, the Christian 'comes off victorious'. This verse is written in the present tense, that is, we are constantly overcoming. See John 17:13-16; Christ would not put us in an impossible position.

Relationship to the Devil - 1 John 3:7-9

Habitual sin is from Satan. Jesus, by His finished work on the Cross, is the means by which the Devil's works are loosened or dissolved; that is, they are brought to no effect. We can know freedom from the various occultic practices that have bound us until now.

Christ has finished the work; we are born of the Spirit that has overcome Satan and his works. We may not necessarily 'feel great', but that is not essential. Just read the Old Testament stories of David, Gideon and in the New Testament, Peter. They did not feel great or that they could 'do it' but they were available and ready to be used by God. We do not need to feel, but we are to meditate on and allow the Spirit of God to reveal the truth of these Scriptures to us.

If we want to help others then we need to have such an experience. Indeed, for many, if they come to know Jesus Christ in such a close way they will find the fear and problems of their occult experiences disappear.

Now that we know where we stand spiritually, we are ready to take step two...

Getting Dressed Properly

In occultic situations, when we are dealing with supernatural evil, we must first put something off - fear. This was the first thing Jehoshaphat had to deal with before his great victory against literal enemies [2 Chronicles 20:3 & 15]. We cannot face our supernatural enemy if we are afraid.

We should build on biblical teaching not just the experience of others. Note 1 John 4:18; the perfect love of God casts out all fear. Putting off fear is accomplished by getting to know the love of God better not by some technique.

Talking of techniques, we should not use them against supernatural evil. If we try to do something that is second-hand, we can be in danger. The sons of Sceva found that out to their cost in Acts 19:14. They were trying to do things third-hand - in the name of Jesus whom Paul preaches - not just second-hand. If we read about a technique in a book, we must first ask the question: is it Biblical? If the answer to that is 'Yes', we must then ask: But can I use it in faith and confidence? Only if we can answer yes to both questions should we move ahead.

God Gives Us Armour

Ephesians 6:10 onwards explains our correct dress for battle. Put on the armour is in the 'Aorist Imperative Tense', which means it is a command to be obeyed at once and once for all. Our battle dress is not just for special occasions, it is every-day clothing!

We are to stand against the schemes of Satan [verse 11]. How can we stand against something we know nothing about? Remember that our struggle is not against flesh and blood [verse 12]. We are not against the people but the power behind the people. However, do note carefully the words that Paul used; sometimes it might be a 'struggle'!

We talked about fear being overcome by getting to know God better and here each part of the armour describes part of the character of God that we need to know in reality. As we do, we will know the active working of the armour. Miss some of them and we will be vulnerable.

- The girdle, the foundation garment, is truth or reality. What is the answer to a lie - truth! What is the answer to a deception - the reality! The very foundation garment that God gives us deals with one of the main weapons and characteristics of Satan.

- Righteousness - which is from Christ, not something that we manufacture, is over the heart - the centre of our emotions. As we know the reality of this, we are allowing our actions to be energised by the Holy

Spirit's righteous acts and not by our own good ideas. We are not just moved emotionally but we are discovering what God says about something.

- The sandals of a Roman soldier gave him firm footing in the battle. We obviously need that in our lives, and here that is described as the basics of the gospel. How we need to understand, for example, justification and sanctification so we have a reality about the gospel we believe and are able to stand firm against the lies and taunts of Satan.

- The large shield, which in those days would have been about four foot high and two and half foot wide typifies our faith. We can be secure and have complete trust in the Lord and His works.

- Salvation is over our heads so that our minds are not carried away with some great man-made scheme or train of thought. We know the reality and security of our God and what He has delivered us from and indeed what He has brought us into.

- The sword is the Word of God not for slashing around but to be used expertly under the Holy Spirit's direction.

We need to be continually meditating on these aspects of the armour so that the Lord can show us increasingly what it means for us.

Having passed stages one and two, we are ready to understand in a little more detail what happens to someone who opens the door to the occult.

Demon Possession

The Greek word found in the four Gospels is *daimonzomai*, which literally means 'demonisation', that is, the way we are affected by demonic or satanic forces. Satan, although a supernatural being, cannot be everywhere as God can, and that is why he has such a well-run army [Ephesians 6:12]. In order for any of these beings to affect us inwardly, they need a doorway through which to enter. Satan was looking for such a doorway when he tempted Jesus [Luke 4:1-13]. He tempted Jesus on every level - body, soul and spirit - but no doorway was found and he had to leave and wait for a more opportune time.

We usually talk about oppression or possession, but Scripture shows the satanic realm is affecting the person. Do not, however, fall into the trap of believing that everything is a demon - there is the world and flesh to be considered, too. Each case must be taken on its own merit. If the flesh is the problem, then an understanding of 'death to self' is vital. We would need to know the reality of Jesus delivering us from the power of habitual sin and not all the time giving in and pampering our flesh. If it's the world that is a problem, then we need to ask the Lord to reveal to us the reality of what it means to deny ourselves and take up our cross.

If we try to cast out a demon that is not there, we can cause one of two extreme problems. Either the person does not bother to change, because it is not their fault, but the demon's. Alternatively, they become laden with guilt and fear because they have a demon that will not come out.

The way the person acts is not always a clear indication. There will be those who are demonised and will respond in a violent way when the name of Jesus is used or someone talks about the blood of Jesus. However, there will be others who do not. In some cases in Scripture, it appears the demonised said good things, for example, Luke 4:31&41 or Acts 16:17. It was not what they were saying but the spirit in which they were saying it that was the indication. Other indications of demonisation could be bondage, compulsions, darkness of personality (especially in the eyes), suicidal tendencies, severe nightmares. These are the outworkings of the character of the one to whom they have opened up.

Can a Christian Be Possessed?

Some will say the answer must be yes because of the number we read of in the Bible who were 'possessed'. But this leaves out the important fact that they were not born again. The answer actually depends on what the enquirer means by 'possessed'. If I am a Christian the Holy Spirit must fill my spirit, at least in measure, and as such, I cannot be possessed. However, if the question is, can a Christian be afflicted by a demon? The answer is "yes". I can open a doorway and allow my life to be affected and some form of deliverance will be needed.

A perfect illustration of this is found in Peter's life (Matthew16:23) where he allowed Satan to impose his will on him and he needed Jesus' rebuke. This had an even greater fulfilment when Peter denied the Lord at the crucifixion.

Whether talking to our friends and neighbours or witnessing to strangers, we will find those who are involved with the occult. We need some in our church, village or town, who are prepared, and able, to help such ones.

Now we are ready to start helping others - but how?

Build Bridges

Build bridges of love, not brick walls of accusation. Do not immediately condemn the person simply because he or she believes something different from you. Find out what they were looking for and why they got involved with the particular group or practice. Do not be afraid to share your testimony of what Jesus has done for you, but do not be a 'raving evangelical loony'; rather show love and compassion.

Never overstate your case. If you say, 'Everyone who has played with the Ouija board is demon possessed', you will lose credibility because it is just not true. Only say what you can back up with fact.

Use Apologetics

The word 'apologetics' sometimes puts people off but it is a great word. Apologetics means making a reasoned defence of what we believe and why. We do not just use Biblical phrases that the 'man in the street' does not understand but we explain those phrases in words and illustrations he does understand. A presentation to someone involved in an occult practice could go something like this.

A human has no inherent supernatural power. The moment that something happens beyond the natural, it must come from one of the two sources of supernatural power. Even the events in this world show that there are two opposing forces. Which one is the source of the power you are experiencing: good or evil? Is it from God Who wants to set you free, or from Satan who wants to snare and trap you? Just because 'It works' does not mean that it is okay to use.

We must check back to the source for a very good reason. The supernatural is more powerful than 'me' in the natural. Am I therefore opening my life up to something that is not only more powerful than I am, but that also wants to do me harm? One question that sums all this up is, 'Who holds the copyright on the practice I am involved with?'

God condemns certain practices in Scripture; thus they cannot have their source in Him. Deuteronomy 18:9-14 lists most occultic practices that people get involved in today. These are described as.

- Passing through fire - initiation ceremonies and sacrifice

- Divination - discovery of the future by supernatural means

- Witchcraft - use of hidden arts - i.e., occultic

- Interprets omens - prognosticates - foretells - e.g. palmistry, teacups etc.

- Sorcerer - practise magic spells

- Casts spells - specific magic that binds up - a charmer

- Medium - consults familiar spirits

- Spiritualist - a knowing one - always used in a bad sense

- Calls up the dead - a necromancer who consults the dead.

God clearly forbids us to be involved in any such practices. Is He mean in giving us this restrictive command? We all are happy to have certain restrictions in our lives. There is one law that we are all very happy about - driving on the left-hand side of the road. Why are we happy about such a restrictive law? It stops chaos and death. That is exactly what God is doing here. He forbids us to be involved in these things because He knows the chaos and death that result. He is being a God of freedom, not restriction, because He wants us to have the best. God knows these other practices come from the evil spirits and does not want us to suffer at their hands.

Ministering Deliverance

If we, or someone we are dealing with, has been or is being affected in some way by the Satanic realm, we need to close the door and receive the Lord's cleansing and filling by the Holy Spirit.

With the occult there may be times, as recorded in Scripture, when we can command the spirit to leave the person without any co-operation on their part. However, in practice, there usually needs to be co-operation. The person co-operates by repenting and turning their back on the practice that opened the doorway in the first place.

There is no A-Z of deliverance but below we summarise some main areas that will probably need to be covered.

First, a few basic pointers for counselling or helping someone. If this is something that you will be doing on a regular basis, we suggest that you take a proper counselling course to highlight these and many other important points.

- Always work with at least one other person unless it is impossible. There is strength in fellowship and while one is counselling the other can be praying.

- Never, unless impossible, counsel a member of the opposite sex without someone being with you. If a man must counsel a woman, ensure that there is another female Christian with you.

- It is advisable to keep a good clear record of what was said and was suggested.

Now we will highlight some points that should be considered by the helper or counsellor.

- Build a bridge to the person in love as Jesus did to the Samaritan woman. Do not accuse and condemn but seek to understand why the person is in the position they are. [John 3:16, 17]

- Be real to yourself - do not do anything simply because someone else does it or you read about it somewhere. Ask yourself two questions, 'Is it Scriptural?' and if yes, 'Can I do this in faith?' Only if the answer to both questions is yes should you go ahead.

- Our relationship with the Lord is vital. In Mark 9 after the Lord came down from the Mount of Transfiguration we read of the boy who was demon possessed. The disciples could not help him and in the end [v.29] Jesus says that this sort would not come out except by prayer and fasting. The demon actually came out by the command of the Lord; I believe, therefore, that prayer and fasting are to deepen our relationship with the Lord so that we are ready for such challenges.

- Ensure that any fear in our hearts or minds is dealt with and we have peace about what we are doing.

- Listen with the heart, our innermost being, not just with the head. It can be that it is not what is said but, either what is behind the words used or, indeed, what is not said, that is the key. Some come just pretending to have been involved in these things to receive attention - listening carefully will often reveal this.

- Do not always jump to the conclusion that there is satanic influence and a spirit needs to be cast out. Sometimes it is discipline needed in the person's life.

- If we are aware that there is satanic influence, seek to find the point of entry - how have they opened the door to this influence in their lives? Revelation 2:4.5 tells us that the Christians in Ephesus had to remember from where they had fallen. We see this principle in Abraham's life too, after going down into Egypt - he returned to the exact place he left. Finding the opening where Satan came in is often very helpful, although not necessarily vital.

- Do note the simplicity of Jesus in Luke 4:35 & 8:33. It may not be possible for us to be always as simple and efficient, but we do not need to over-complicate matters. One school of thought wants to make deliverance a science that needs a PhD but the KISS (Keep it Simple Stupid) principle is still, I believe, the best.

I Want To Be Set Free

What about the one being helped; how do they need to co-operate?

- First, they need to come to a place of confession and repentance of their past involvement. They need to renounce the system they got involved in. [James 4:4]. In addition, it helps if they see that the blood and sacrifice of Jesus Christ are sufficient to forgive and deliver them from the past. Sometimes it helps to declare this fact aloud through Scriptures such as Revelation 12:11, Ephesians 1:7. Romans 5:9, and Hebrews 13:12.

- Strong and specific prayer can then be made to resist the devil, based on James 4:7. Do note, however, that our authority to resist him comes when the life is brought under the control of the Lord by repentance and confession. My personal belief is that it is dangerous to seek to perform deliverance without the person being willing to put their life under the Lord's sovereignty. Will anything actually change in the long-term? Will not Satan simply return because the doorway is still open?

- Once the demonic influence has been resisted and it has left, then the open doorway needs to be closed. Just as the Children of Israel needed to close the door on their wanderings in the wilderness - Joshua 5:2-9 - we need to make strong prayer and supplication to the grace and mercy of God to close the door, now that repentance has been made.

- This is not the end, though, because now there is a vacuum in the life. Ask the Holy Spirit to come and fill every 'nook and cranny' of the area that is empty.

- This is still only the beginning — the person needs to be willing to lay a foundation of basic doctrine in their lives; and, too, commit themselves to a loving and understanding church or fellowship that can continue this process.

Group Activity

1. Write in your own words what you think being a Christian means.

2. If a friend says they are affected by supernatural evil, what advice would you give them? This could either be achieved in discussion or by acting out a drama scene.

3. Make a model or picture of a Christian wearing the armour mentioned in Ephesians 6. The finished object should not need any explanation as to what each piece of armour is, but it should be clear just by looking at the model or picture. Then discuss what each one needs to do to ensure they know the reality of the armour in their lives.

Follow-Up

Once deliverance has taken place, it is often the beginning of a new way of life and the need to cultivate new 'habits' and priorities in our daily living. Think carefully about the following Scriptures, and see how they come into this category. Write out a sentence beside each of these verses to highlight what help there can be in our life to maintaining our freedom. Spend time praying and seeking the Lord as to how these should be worked out in your own life. There may also be many other relevant verses that you can find.

Conclusion

The ones below are in chronological order, not necessarily a priority order for your life; indeed, in time, we will need to see the reality of all these truths.

Psalm 119:9-11
Acts 2:42
1 Corinthians 10:13
Ephesians 5:18-21
Colossians 2:6-10
James 4:7